THE BEDFORD SERIES IN HISTORY AND CULTURE

Thomas Edison
and Modern America

A Brief History with Documents

Related Titles in
THE BEDFORD SERIES IN HISTORY AND CULTURE
Advisory Editors: Lynn Hunt, *University of California, Los Angeles*
David W. Blight, *Yale University*
Bonnie G. Smith, *Rutgers University*
Natalie Zemon Davis, *Princeton University*
Ernest R. May, *Harvard University*

THE BEDFORD SERIES IN HISTORY AND CULTURE

Thomas Edison and Modern America

A Brief History with Documents

Theresa M. Collins

Thomas A. Edison Papers, *Rutgers University*

and

Lisa Gitelman

Catholic University of America

with

Gregory Jankunis

Thomas A. Edison Papers, *Rutgers University*

BEDFORD/ST. MARTIN'S   Boston ♦ New York

For Bedford/St. Martin's
Publisher for History: Patricia A. Rossi
Director of Development for History: Jane Knetzger
Developmental Editor: Sarah Barrash Wilson
Editorial Assistant: Julie Mooza
Editorial Assistant, Publishing Services: Maria Teresa Burwell
Senior Production Supervisor: Joe Ford
Marketing Manager: Jenna Bookin Barry
Project Management: Books By Design, Inc.
Indexer: Books By Design, Inc.
Text Design: Claire Seng-Niemoeller
Cover Design: Richard Emery Design, Inc.
Cover Photo: Thomas Edison, Courtesy of the U.S. Department of the Interior, the
    National Park Service, Edison National Historic Site.
Composition: Stratford Publishing Services, Inc.
Printing and Binding: Haddon Craftsmen, an RR Donnelley & Sons Company

President: Charles H. Christensen
Editorial Director: Joan E. Feinberg
Director of Marketing: Karen R. Melton
Director of Editing, Design, and Production: Marcia Cohen
Manager, Publishing Services: Emily Berleth

Library of Congress Control Number: 2001098228

Manufactured in the United States of America.

1 0 9 8 7
f   e   d   c   b

For information, write: Bedford/St. Martin's, 75 Arlington Street, Boston, MA 02116
(617-399-4000)

ISBN-10: 0-312-24734-6 (paperback)
          0-312-29476-X (hardcover)
ISBN-13: 978-0-312-24734-8 (paperback)
          978-0-312-29476-2 (hardcover)

Acknowledgments
Page 86: Archives of the Pierpont Morgan Library, New York. J. Pierpont Morgan, *Letter
to Walter Burns.*
Unless otherwise noted, the documents exist in the archive of the Edison National
Historic Site and appear courtesy of the National Park Service, the U.S. Department of
the Interior.

Foreword

The Bedford Series in History and Culture is designed so that readers can study the past as historians do.

The historian's first task is finding the evidence. Documents, letters, memoirs, interviews, pictures, movies, novels, or poems can provide facts and clues. Then the historian questions and compares the sources. There is more to do than in a courtroom, for hearsay evidence is welcome, and the historian is usually looking for answers beyond act and motive. Different views of an event may be as important as a single verdict. How a story is told may yield as much information as what it says.

Along the way the historian seeks help from other historians and perhaps from specialists in other disciplines. Finally, it is time to write, to decide on an interpretation and how to arrange the evidence for readers.

Each book in this series contains an important historical document or group of documents, each document a witness from the past and open to interpretation in different ways. The documents are combined with some element of historical narrative—an introduction or a biographical essay, for example—that provides students with an analysis of the primary source material and important background information about the world in which it was produced.

Each book in the series focuses on a specific topic within a specific historical period. Each provides a basis for lively thought and discussion about several aspects of the topic and the historian's role. Each is short enough (and inexpensive enough) to be a reasonable one-week assignment in a college course. Whether as classroom or personal reading, each book in the series provides firsthand experience of the challenge—and fun—of discovering, recreating, and interpreting the past.

Lynn Hunt
David W. Blight
Bonnie G. Smith
Natalie Zemon Davis
Ernest R. May

Preface

Though best remembered for his role in electrification, the American inventor Thomas Alva Edison (1847–1931) was actually involved with the many interdependent processes that collectively constitute modernization. Edison's varied participation in the course of industrialization, urbanization, and globalization is also evident in a rich documentary legacy, for he left behind an archive of more than 5 million items, making his career a particularly good place for historians to glimpse the emergence of modern America. In addition, Edison has long been the subject of myth as well as history, so that inquiring into the inception, character, and longevity of Edison's iconic stature in American culture offers one way to gauge the cultural workings of modernization.

This book makes the work of Thomas Edison available to nonspecialists. It includes more than 100 documents, most of them drawn from the archive housed at the Edison National Historic Site in West Orange, New Jersey. We have selected these documents less because they celebrate a single great man and more because they offer an opportunity to look into the concerns of his day and into the forces of change that helped to shape modern America and that remain important in the world today. We encourage readers to gauge for themselves what Edison was like and how he invented, while also inquiring more deeply into the contexts, processes, and interplay of technological innovation and modernization.

The documents are arranged into four thematic chapters. Chapter 1 provides an autobiographical view of Edison and the personal traits of a unique individual who came to symbolize for many the characteristics of his country. Chapter 2 offers a range of perspectives on the events that first made Edison famous, his invention of the phonograph in 1877 and its public introduction in 1878. Chapter 3 collects a variety of documents describing Edison's fabled work on electricity, which resulted in a whole system of electric light and power distribution, and revealing the processes of invention in much of its unfamiliar complexity. Chapter 4 offers a look at some of Edison's later inventions, tracing the inventor's influence more broadly in the media and culture of the 1890s and early twentieth century. Our choice throughout has been to select items for students of American history, although the subject of modernization is one that points beyond such an exclusive, national focus.

ACKNOWLEDGMENTS

The editors wish to acknowledge the continuing work and intellectual legacies of the Thomas A. Edison Papers, a long-term scholarly editing project at Rutgers, the State University of New Jersey. We are grateful as well to our editors at Bedford/St. Martin's, Patricia A. Rossi and Sarah Barrash Wilson, as well as the generous reviewers of our manuscript, Martha J. King, John D. Peters, Carl Prince, Lauren Rabinovitz, and John W. Servos, and the two who remain anonymous. The Program in Media Studies at Catholic University and the Obermann Center for Advanced Studies at the University of Iowa both provided some institutional support for this project. Other crucial and continuous threads in the development of this book were found in discussions with fellow members of the Association for Documentary Editing and in consultations with colleagues from the program in Archival Management and Historical Editing at New York University, especially Esther Katz.

Theresa M. Collins
Lisa Gitelman
Gregory Jankunis

Contents

Illustrations

Thomas Edison and Modern America

A Brief History with Documents

Introduction:
Edison, Invention, and Modernity

Man's thought-machine works just like the other animals, but is a better one and more Edisonian. — Mark Twain, *What Is Man* (1906)

Ask why Thomas A. Edison became an American of greatness, and a likely answer would be, "He invented the electric light bulb." While good for grade-school students or game show contestants, that answer is less than accurate, less than complete. There is more to Edison than light bulbs. He invented and introduced a whole system of incandescent electric lighting; he invented a means to record and replay sound; and he contributed to the development of telegraphs, telephones, motion pictures, and more. Edison obtained more United States patents than any other individual—1,093 in all. His first was issued in 1869, when he was only twenty-two, and his last patent application was filed in 1931, the year of his death. Over those decades Thomas Edison became a symbol of American know-how, a hero who seemed to rise above the messy conflicts that occur during times of change. His lifetime spanned eighty-five years of unparalleled industrialization, urbanization, and economic expansion in America, a time in which many Americans were ambivalent about the frenzied pace of change, and vacillated between enthusiasm and suspicion about it. The figure of Edison helped to affirm that technology was a force uniquely suited to make life better for all. How that occurred is a story of Edison and America intertwined.

Even as he remains rooted in the popular imagination as a symbol of American ingenuity, dogged determination, and success, Thomas Edison can help fashion questions about individualism, about who gets credit for inventions and the ways in which credit is ascribed. He can help frame questions about progress, about how (or, in fact whether) technology advances, and about the necessary contexts for

1

technological change. And he can help frame questions about modernity, about the modern landscape of amusements and conveniences, the media, industry, and infrastructure that continue to condition everyday life today.

CHANGING TIMES

When Thomas Edison was born in 1847, the transcontinental reach of the United States was on the brink of reality, yet most businesses were local affairs, managed by the families that owned them, and only around a million Americans worked in manufacturing. During the 1850s the nation's largely agrarian economy was based in part on westward expansion and in part upon slave labor.

Edison grew to maturity amid three large-scale transformations in the patterns of production and consumption that set the stage for his career. First was the staggering growth of transportation and information networks. Until the 1840s, interpersonal communication depended upon face-to-face meetings or the physical transport of messages. It could take three weeks to travel from New York to Chicago, if the weather was favorable. By 1860 fast, dependable rail service shortened the trip to two days. The train often carried special cars for the mail, but the invention and implementation of telegraphy opened a wholly new dimension: electrical communication.

Telegraphy reconstructed language into coded messages of dots and dashes, which were then transmitted electrically over wires. The signals came over the wire to receiving machines in telegraph offices, where operators transcribed or relayed the messages to other stations in the system. Newspapers were among the first to appreciate the use of telegraphs for receiving and distributing timely information, and armies as well as financiers were also quick to perceive the benefits of rapid communications, but telegraphy found its earliest extensive applications in connection with the railroads. From station to station and switch to switch, telegraphy helped railroad managers build and control the construction and traffic of entire systems. The first transcontinental telegraph connection was established in 1861; a transcontinental rail link came in 1869.

The modern, integrated transportation and communication infrastructure helped to support a second large-scale transformation of American life in the form of a managerial revolution that made giant corporations the dominant feature of the American economy. Manufacturers standardized goods and came to appreciate the economic advantages of large-scale production and interchangeable parts. Flour mills and meat-packing plants pioneered the use of continuous flow production, the precursor to Henry Ford's assembly line of 1914, while vast industrial processes overtook much of the manufacturing that had previously been accomplished by individual craftsmen or by relatively skilled workers in semimechanized mills. Changes appeared beyond the shop floor as well. A few large corporations began to internalize and institutionalize the process of invention in departments of research and development (also known as R&D), which were intended to give them technological advantages over their competitors. Managerial bureaucracies also increasingly supplanted owner-managers, and white-collar workers became the fastest growing segment of the workforce in America.

In addition, Edison's era was party to large-scale transformations in the processes of consumption. The patterns of what people bought and where people bought were shifting, as rural and small-town America grew accustomed to buying merchandise through mail-order catalogs, while city dwellers learned to shop at department stores. With the growth in white-collar jobs, modest increases in middle-class incomes helped to create new opportunities for leisure and material accumulation. By the late 1880s trademarks, brand names, and national advertising campaigns became more common: Western Union meant telegraphy; Bell meant telephones; and Singer meant sewing machines. These big names kept company with other product names, such as Swift (packaged meat), Heinz (pickles and ketchup), Quaker (breakfast cereal), Colt (firearms), Campbell (canned soup), Procter & Gamble (soap), and Eastman Kodak (film and photographic paper). All would contribute to the experience of American consumers over the next century.

Thomas Edison made contributions to all of the changes discussed above. Although he could not cause anything like changes of this magnitude himself, the inventor came to represent modernity, first in the eyes of his contemporaries and then in the eyes of successive generations. By the early twentieth century, Edison was positioned as securely as Christopher Columbus and George Washington in the curriculum of American schoolchildren, and he has remained a comfortably familiar icon of ingenuity. To this day, whenever the news media gather a list of the most important people in American history, Edison is there, often at the top of the list. However thoroughly technological change has altered modern life, the figure of Edison apparently continues to make its chaotic pace more palatable, marking its purpose as a distinctly American one by symbolizing the achievements of the past. Now as then, Edison resolves the contradiction between excelling and representing: he achieved great things, but he was just a regular guy, one who dressed in work clothes, smoked cheap cigars, and got his hands dirty.

THOMAS ALVA EDISON

Thomas Edison was born in Milan, Ohio, on February 11, 1847, in a brick house designed by his father, Samuel. Milan bustled with commerce after a canal connected it with Lake Erie in 1839, and for a while it provided ample opportunities for Samuel Edison to make a trade of his carpentry skills, and dabble in land speculation. But Milan just as quickly found its best years behind it as railroads, not canals, began to dominate commerce. By 1854 the Edison family moved to the outskirts of Port Huron, Michigan, a lumber town on the Canadian border where Samuel tried his hand at several businesses. The family also farmed, growing produce for their table and for sale. As an additional source of income they rented rooms to boarders, and at one point they charged curiosity seekers to view the bustling port from an observation deck Samuel built in the family's yard.

Not much is known for sure about Edison's youth, despite a long tradition of anecdotal appreciations. The most recent scholarship challenges the established mythology, suggesting, for instance, that Edison may have been home schooled to save the cost of tuition and not, as previous accounts suggest, because he was sickly, inattentive, or addled. His mother, Mary, was a former schoolteacher, who probably made his education another of her household chores. Recent scholarship similarly questions whether Edison's partial deafness might have originated from a childhood illness and not, as lore has had it, as the result of having his ears boxed by an angry train conductor.[1]

When Edison himself recalled the events of his boyhood, he never produced a complete or continuous narrative. Instead, snippets of personal reminiscence and anecdotes were repeated and elaborated in newspapers and biographies, so that the otherwise ordinary activities of Edison's boyhood took on extraordinary significance in the context of his later accomplishments. His stories tended to present a youngster who was as hardworking as he was bold and curious, an

[1]See Paul Israel, *Edison: A Life of Invention* (New York: John Wiley & Sons, 1998).

entrepreneur-in-the-making, who connected with a generalized sense of America as a young nation. He recalled seeing immigrant trains loaded with Scandinavian settlers on their way to the Great Plains, for instance. He was also drawn to the railroad depot in Port Huron, which became his point of entry into the world of work beyond his parents' home. At fourteen years of age, Edison climbed aboard the local train to peddle newspapers, snacks, and similar merchandise. He soon after opened stands to sell periodicals, fruits, and produce in Port Huron. Bringing in a few baskets of vegetables daily from Detroit, his cargo was loaded on the mail car of the train, and carried off the books, if not for free, since the conductors who turned a blind eye to this infraction of company rules seemed to get produce at discount in return.

Edison learned from his experiences, both good and bad. For example, he closed the periodical stand when he felt his employee could not be trusted. In a happier instance, he made a large profit one day during 1862, while selling newspapers on the Grand Trunk Railway. As the story goes, he realized that demand for a breaking story about the Civil War battle of Shiloh would outstrip his normal supply of papers, so he arranged for credit, to get more newspapers than he could afford to buy. He then sold the papers at increasingly higher prices at every station stop along the way, charging whatever the market for war news would bear.

That spring Edison started his own newspaper, called the *Weekly Herald*. The only extant issue contains stories about railroad engineers and porters, as well as schedules for stagecoaches and horse-drawn omnibuses, among other means to make travel connections with the rails. He also printed "a peep at things generally," offering a touch of intrigue in the story of a swindle gone awry, and one item of humor, which was slipped mischievously under the title of "News." Edison produced the paper in the baggage car of the train, alongside a small chemical laboratory, where he experimented, until a mishap with his chemicals caused a fire, and he was forced to relocate the laboratory to the cellar of his parents' home. Another nearly serious accident from these days was possibly a myth, but it became a signature, life-changing event that set Edison on his path to greatness. One day Edison saw a little boy in the path of an oncoming train and pulled him to safety; to express his appreciation, the child's father introduced young Edison to the secrets of telegraphy.

Clichés jump from stories such as these, which tend to make the boy Edison into a virtual Horatio Alger character, with enough luck and pluck so that patience and industry are the wellspring of success. The real story to be gleaned from his early life may be less what really happened than how each episode retrospectively fit into the legend of an American hayseed who made good through a combination of native intelligence and homespun, "golden rule" morals. Whether strictly true or not, episodes in Edison's youth replayed the autobiographies of heroes like Benjamin Franklin and Abraham Lincoln, while they resonated powerfully with an affirmative ideology about America as the land of opportunity.

Whatever his immediate stimulus, at the age of fifteen Edison began to study and practice telegraphy in earnest. He was aware that thousands of miles of wire already connected the nation, and that the telegraph was used to coordinate rail traffic, to communicate news, and to conduct business. Most important, telegraphy was indispensable to military strategy, as both sides of the then-raging Civil War were using telegraphs to coordinate the movement of troops, supplies, and intelligence. Edison easily found opportunities to work in the world of telegraphy, since operators often were in short supply during and immediately after the war, but at least one twist made his technique as a telegraph operator unusual. Edison was already hard of hearing, and telegraph receiving instruments of the day were "sounders" or acoustic instruments. The average operator listened to the clicking and tapping, then transcribed the dots and dashes of Morse code into written text; Edison would have had to watch and feel the electrical impulses, while others relied more upon their sounds. He would also invent one of the first printing telegraphs in 1869.

Edison left home in 1863. Over the next five years he worked, trained, studied, and experimented in telegraphy at various locations. Employed first at tiny stations around Michigan and Ontario, he later worked at various offices of the Western Union Telegraph Company, which had built the first transcontinental telegraph line and was nearly a monopoly in America's telegraph industry. As Edison moved about, through Indianapolis, Cincinnati, Memphis, and Louisville, he became initiated into the informal fraternity of young, white men who frequently moved from office to office, but whose facility with the telegraph instrument or "key" assured them a job wherever they went. The best operators were highly skilled and sometimes engaged in improving telegraph technology. Several became Edison's friends and mentors, encouraged his experimental work, looked over his sketches, and helped him build and try new devices. By the time Edison arrived in Cincinnati, he was barely sixteen years of age, but already a proficient telegrapher and sharp at the key when copying messages off the wire. He worked day and night, finding time to read technical literature and develop his experimental techniques with regard to the electrical, mechanical, and chemical components of telegraphy. One object of fascination to him was the repeater, which could relay messages automatically, over longer distances. Another was multiple telegraphy, or multiplex telegraphy, the capacity to pass more than one message over a wire at a time. He also worked on printing telegraphs and specialized telegraphs that served as fire alarms.

Although common wisdom called for ambitious young men to go west, in 1868 Edison instead headed east to Boston, where he positioned himself among the elite of telegraph operators—technicians who contributed to improving the design of machines and systems. He published a few articles about his own inventions in the *Telegrapher,* the official journal of the National Telegraph Union. By January 1869, he had found an ally to finance the introduction of his printing telegraphs, which were hotly desired for reporting up-to-date quotations on the prices of stocks and gold. Edison resigned from his job as a telegraph operator in order to become a full-time inventor. He went to New York City in April 1869, to help one of Western Union's competitors test a telegraph connection with Buffalo, and in June his first two patents were issued, one for an electric vote recorder (never successful) and the other for printing telegraphy. In August, a leading enterprise in providing financial news services made Edison its superintendent. Although this was a considerable leap of stature, Edison's tenure with the firm was short-lived, and he soon moved to Newark, New Jersey, a port and manufacturing town.

He next established a number of jointly owned enterprises and continued his experiments at several workshops in succession. The variety and pace of his alliances indicate that Edison struggled to find congenial working conditions, a suitably equipped place to work, and the capital to proceed. Along the way he hired several dozen workmen and assistants. He briefly pursued a business called the News Reporting Telegraph Company, which offered its subscribers "all general news of the world . . . in advance of all newspapers." Most traces of the firm soon vanished, except that Mary Stilwell, a sixteen-year-old girl employed by the company, became Edison's wife on December 25, 1871. Apparently in anticipation of his forthcoming nuptial, Edison had bought a house in Newark during the previous month. In February 1873, their first child was born—a daughter named Marion. Work preoccupied Edison after his marriage, just as it had previously. In the months and years after his wedding, Edison was completely immersed in the invention, testing, and manufacture of high-speed automatic telegraphy, chemical and mechanical printers, and additional matters related to telegraphy. Two months after the birth of his daughter, business beckoned abroad. Edison headed to England, where his "universal stock ticker" was already in use at the Exchange Telegraph Company of London, to demonstrate his automatic telegraph system for the British Post Office.

Edison's breakthroughs with various versions of the stock ticker dazzled investors and earned him repute as an inventor. The subsequent contracts enlarged his inventive and manufacturing capacities, as well as increasing his personal income, although his expenses often seemed to outstrip his resources. Edison never seemed to have quite enough money, technical staff, laborers, or equipment to keep pace with his ideas. His contacts with leading executives in the industry were widening, however, and at the beginning of 1873, his labors in the field of multiple telegraphy paid off. When Edison showed his designs to William Orton, president of Western Union, the inventor gained access to that company's facilities for making and testing experimental apparatus. Western Union had already embraced an improved system of duplex telegraphy, invented by Joseph Stearns, and it had practically doubled the company's ability to carry messages without adding the cost of new wires and their maintenance. Orton's interest in Edison lay in the hope that the young inventor would discover potential breakthroughs in multiple telegraphy, so that Western Union could control any new development that otherwise might undermine its current advantage.

In 1874 Edison successfully developed a "quadruplex" telegraph, exactly the kind of innovation that Orton had anticipated and desired. It would handle four messages over the same wire, carrying two in each direction at once. But because Orton's understanding with Edison was never put in writing, Edison was free to offer his invention to Western Union's arch rival, the Atlantic and Pacific Telegraph Company, controlled by the brilliantly ruthless financier and railroad magnate, Jay Gould. Gould was a singularly controversial figure of the Gilded Age, whose personal fortune at the time was perhaps as much as $25 million, and who was determined to undercut Western Union's dominance. He paid Edison the astronomical sum of $30,000 for the quadruplex. However, whatever hard feelings there might have been, Orton continued to respect Edison's technical ingenuity, and, in an attempt to be sure that his oversight was not repeated, Orton established a contractual relationship with the inventor, making him a paid consultant for Western Union. The contract provided a weekly salary and future royalties for Edison, an independent inventor, in exchange for the exclusive rights to those inventions that could be used on the land lines of telegraphs or upon cables in the United States.

Edison had employed as many as 120 workers in 1874, but there was never enough time or money to pursue his own ideas fully. By early 1876, however, his profits from the quadruplex were already on the account books, and his improved "electric pen" (a stenciling device used to make multiple copies of business documents) was bringing additional income. The inventor finally seemed to have sufficient financial resources to establish his own laboratory, with a pared down team of fewer than twenty associates. Toward the end of 1875, Edison decided to retreat from urban life and devote himself to experimental work exclusively. In early 1876 he moved with his family and a select team of technicians and craftsmen to the small village of Menlo Park, New Jersey, where he transformed a cluster of buildings into a state-of-the-art experimental complex, including his own electrical and chemical laboratories, machine shop, and library. An isolated place, Menlo Park offered cheaper land and fewer interruptions than the city. It answered Edison's need for an environment in which he could fully investigate and develop his ideas. Yet it was also near enough to New York so that he and his associates could meet clients and invite journalists and investors to visit when Edison wanted to demonstrate his latest breakthrough.

During his first months at Menlo Park, Edison was preparing to exhibit the best of his inventive output at the U.S. Centennial Exhibition, scheduled to open during May 1876 in Philadelphia. A few weeks into the exhibition, Alexander Graham Bell demonstrated his astonishing new twist on acoustic telegraphy, the telephone, which allowed the electrical transmission of speech. Whereas most people reacted to Bell's telephone with absolute amazement, Edison and the men at Western Union more quickly noted its imperfections, for Bell's earliest device did not work very well. After so many years spent on improving the printing telegraphs, there were even some who dismissed Bell's telephone as a "scientific toy," since it did not result in a printed message and was therefore, presumably, of less value to the needs of business clients. Even the critics, however, were not above envy, as they were meanwhile eyeing the lucrative possibilities of Bell's discovery, and maneuvering to develop it for their own benefit.

That autumn Edison intensively honed his efforts toward improving Bell's device, while at the same time trying to invent around Bell's patents, in order to secure for himself and Western Union some of the valuable intellectual property being developed in the new field of telephony. Patents, simply put, are legal documents that protect inventors' rights to the new inventions they specify. Any unspecified improvement made by someone else is fair game. So Edison and his rivals all tried to outdo each other with new and, they always hoped, crucial improvements to each other's machines. Over the course of these efforts Edison became a household name, except that his fame did not result from his contributions to improvements in telephony. Although Edison's carbon transmitter helped to make the telephone a more practical device for general use, it was for his own astonishingly new device, called the phonograph, that the press dubbed him a "Napoleon of Science" and the "Wizard of Menlo Park."

The first phonograph was very primitive: a rotating cylinder, wrapped with a piece of metal foil, upon which the vibrations of sound were etched by a stylus and thus "captured," Edison said, so they could be replayed later at will. It was not an electronic communication device, but it printed voices in a way the telephone could not. It caused a sensation. Everyone wanted a glimpse of the speaking machine. In 1878 Edison demonstrated his device to the National Academy of Science, to members of Congress, and then to President Rutherford B. Hayes, who invited him to the White House. As one of his promoters gleefully reported, "School girls write compositions on Edison. The funny papers publish squibs on Edison. . . . The daily papers write up his life." Edison himself was delighted to capture the public eye and more than willing to cultivate the attention. From that time on, whatever Thomas Edison did, the newspapers duly took note. It helped that he understood the power of the press and greeted its representatives convivially, with plain talk and exuberant demonstrations of his nascent inventions, often long before they were ready for commercial introduction.

As Edison worked in Menlo Park, the country seemed unable to break free of a severe economic depression that began in 1873. The election of 1876 brought a constitutional crisis, as the Democratic and Republican parties both claimed victory in the presidential election. The price for ending the stalemate brought a halt to Reconstruction in 1877, a year that proved to be the nadir of the long depression and that pushed the United States to the brink of chaos. Economic woes forced railroad companies to cut the wages of their workers by 10

THE WIZARD'S SEARCH.

The Wizard, New York Daily Graphic *(1879)* The newspapers dubbed Edison "The Wizard of Menlo Park" and the name stuck. Here he is pictured in his search for supplies of platinum to use in his incandescent lamp. His hat and gown are covered with pictures of his early inventions.

Courtesy of the Edison National Historic Site, National Park Service, U.S. Department of the Interior.

percent, causing workers to strike, occupy rail yards, and effectively paralyze rail traffic in the United States. The first national strike in America put rifled militiamen face-to-face with angry, hungry laborers and their sympathizers. In city after city there were riotous confrontations between the militias and labor, until President Hayes authorized U.S. Army troops to put down the insurrection.

In the context of such strife, the figures of inventors like Edison and Bell sounded a reassuring note. Men like them were hailed as heroes. Their dazzling achievements suggested a better, shared future, guaranteed by technological change, which was dressed up and saluted as "progress," a hopeful abstraction to answer any doubts about the future.

As profiled in the press, inventors were great men who affirmed the values of American individualism. Edison handily helped to advance such ideals by saying that you only needed a tiny bit of inspiration and a whole lot of perspiration to succeed, and at times the unsuspecting public was lulled into thinking that anything was possible, no matter how absurd, if Edison was working on it. Consequently, after a newspaper in New York ran a story for April Fools' Day that claimed "Edison Invents a Machine That Will Feed the Human Race," the idea was spread uncritically by other papers, leading readers to believe the story was fact rather than farce. Edison nevertheless continued to startle the world with the practical possibilities of technology. He did so again by boldly announcing in September 1878 that he would introduce a new form of incandescent lighting.

It was something of an exaggeration, or at least a premature pronouncement, because Edison was speaking merely out of confidence that a few of his ideas would lead to a practical system of electrical lighting. So widespread was his acclaim on the heels of his phonograph that his electrical pronouncement caused a panic in the London stock markets that were trading the shares of gas utility companies. The gas companies were the potential casualties of an electrical system replacing gaslights. Edison wanted to produce incandescent light, in which electricity passes through a filament causing it to glow (or to "incandesce"). If someone could figure out a way to generate electricity efficiently and to get small amounts of it to pass through the right kind of filament under the right conditions, then incandescent electric lamps might be a suitable replacement for gas lamps as a form of illumination in homes, offices, and factories. Other inventors were working on the same thing, and the problem wasn't a simple one: The few experimental generators in existence were woefully inefficient, no one knew how to "subdivide" electricity into manageable increments, and filaments were then called "burners" because electricity passing through them burned them up in an instant. Edison started with the filament problem. Drawing on his work in telegraphy and electromagnetism, he thought he could design a way to regulate the current being fed into a filament. Just as the filament was about to burn up, an automatic regulating device would stop the flow of electricity to let the filament cool. When it had cooled and was starting to lose its glow, the regulating device would complete the circuit again. He worked feverishly with burners and regulators of every conceivable form throughout the autumn of 1878, during the winter and into the spring of 1879. Meanwhile he was drumming up financial support. He was confident. He started to work on generators.

In the course of their research, Edison and his assistants came to several important realizations. They soon knew that they were looking for a filament possessing a high electrical resistance and a small surface area, which would allow the distribution or "subdivision" of current across many parallel circuits, so that individual bulbs or components could be on or off without affecting the whole system. Edison and his assistants also thought they needed a material as durable as platinum, which seemed the best material at first, in spite of its high cost. They gradually realized that automatic regulating devices were not going to work, and beginning in January 1879, Edison began to think in terms of filaments placed inside of sealed bulbs from which the air had been removed, because nothing burns without air. Two key problems remained. First, creating a sufficient vacuum was impossible with the equipment of the day, and second, finding the appropriate filament for such a bulb.

Like several other researchers before them, Edison and his assistants soon understood that carbon made the best filament material. It had none of the durability of platinum or nickel, but it would be safe inside an evacuated glass bulb. Months of work led finally not only to a workable bulb, but also to the component parts of a workable system. Nonetheless, the question of Edison's contribution in the field of electric lighting would often revolve around his originality in designing the bulbs. Other inventors had tried a vacuum, had figured out the need for high resistance, and had used carbon before he did. Indeed, many arguments could be had over whether Edison actually invented a new technology. What Edison invented lay in how he drew together the parts and wholes of a system that worked, designing a place to "plug in" those first workable bulbs, the processes to make them, the generators to power them, while also stringing the wires, connecting the fuses, and figuring out how to measure the current (so they could charge money for it).[2]

Any debate concerning Edison's originality is both suggestive of the competitive contests that regularly occur in the technological marketplace, and indicative of the excitement that surrounded the introduction of electric lighting. Moses Farmer, William Sawyer, Hiram Stevens Maxim, and Joseph Swan all worked to develop incandescent lamps, exhibiting their inventions to the same forums and investors as Edison, who unveiled his electrical lighting system at Menlo Park on December 31, 1879. Edison subsequently offered demonstrations in London and Paris yet chose to perfect every detail of a reliable system before installing a fully operational service. Other rivals were meanwhile installing a related technology for outdoor electrical illumination, called arc lighting, which was much brighter than incandescent bulbs. Arc lighting already lit the night sky at amusement parks, among other urban spaces, and, while Edison worked feverishly to complete his incandescent system, Charles Brush's brilliant arc lights were installed in New York City, making Broadway the "Great White Way." Hiram Maxim and Joseph Swan were meanwhile developing and demonstrating their own versions of incandescent lamps, raising doubts among investors as to whether Edison's incandescent lighting was much different. By the time Edison finally opened the first central power station to generate electricity in lower Manhattan in 1882, there was abundant debate concerning the uniqueness of his claims. There was also widespread anticipation that a new era was opening for electrical illumination, which would "light up mankind from China to Peru." Those who sought to introduce the most practical, accepted form of electrical lighting would also fight to protect their intellectual property, wanting to lay claim to the singular originality of their ideas, and, when necessary, seeking ways to discredit the innovations of rival inventors.

The system that Edison developed was different from his competitors, yet there were also some striking similarities among the various inventors' approaches. The Englishman Joseph Wilson Swan, for instance, had labored intermittently on incandescent lighting since

---

[2]This is the assessment arrived at by the United States judiciary, when it evaluated Edison's patent claims in *Edison Electric Light Company versus United States Electric Lighting Company* in 1891. It is also the interpretation richly documented in *Edison's Electric Light: Biography of an Invention,* the book by Robert Friedel and Paul Israel with Bernard S. Finn (New Brunswick: Rutgers University Press, 1986).

1848. Swan displayed a lamp in December 1879 that closely foreshadowed Edison's design, using a carbon filament, vacuum chamber, and glass bulb. Also like Edison, Swan relied on a combination of particularly useful new scientific discoveries, including the vacuum pump devised in 1855 by German glassblower and instrument maker Heinrich Geissler, which was improved by Heinrich Sprengel in the 1860s. Such pumps were among several key reasons why Thomas Edison succeeded, as his team developed a Geissler-Sprengel pump that was superior to the one used by Swan and capable of making a better vacuum for more effective lamps. Likewise, the English scientist, Michael Faraday had discovered the principles of electrical generation in 1831, and by the mid-1870s dynamos could convert motion into electricity. Much the same as Charles Brush before him, Edison began testing the best machines then available on the world market. These included the generator designed by the Belgian-born Frenchman Zenobe Gramme, as well as a dynamo made by the Siemens company in Germany, and generators from William Wallace of Connecticut, which had been developed in collaboration with Edison rival Moses Farmer. Each was practical for various purposes, but none fully suited Edison's needs. In the process of testing them, Edison and his team also learned how they worked, then modified various elements. They soon produced a more efficient dynamo called the "Jumbo" (it weighed 27 tons) that could generate up to 100 kilowatts and illuminate up to 1,200 lights.

Only fifteen associates were on hand at Menlo Park when Edison began his electric light "campaign," as he called it. By 1881 the laboratory staff at Menlo Park consisted of more than eighty men. An additional forty men worked in the nearby lamp factory, which began production during the summer of 1880. Several among Edison's closest co-workers had worked with him in Newark, including his dedicated laboratory associate from England, Charles Batchelor; his accountant, William Carman, and the master machinist and shop foreman, John Kruesi. Others on the team had joined Edison's enterprise over the course of his electric light research, including the instrument maker and glassblower Ludwig Boehm (also spelled Bohm), a craftsman who had worked with Geissler in Germany. Edison also hired a German chemist, Alfred Haid, a college graduate. A few others on Edison's team had graduated from college, including the mathematic-minded American, Francis Upton, but most of the workers at Menlo Park, like Edison himself, learned and sharpened their skills on the job. By late summer 1880, as many as thirty-five workers were employed at the laboratory in assorted skilled and unskilled roles. They did a variety of jobs, if not always under Edison's direct observation, at least in response to his creative mind, his singular authority, and his motivation. The laboratory work was notably intense, often running round-the-clock, as Edison characteristically worked with little sleep. The routine was punctuated by jokes and pranks, through which the inventor intuitively kept morale high, despite the physically grueling and mentally taxing work. Edison's "muckers," as he eventually called his crew, generally shared a sense of pride and anticipation. In hindsight, many who assisted Edison felt privileged to be working with the charismatic Wizard.

Away from Menlo Park, a variety of important allies were also backing Edison. These included Wall Street attorney Grosvenor P. Lowrey, who represented Western Union. Lowrey proved crucial in assembling a blue-chip roster of venture capitalists to finance the development of Edison's electric lighting system. Among the emerging investors was Hamilton McKay Twombly, whose father-in-law was railroad heir William K. Vanderbilt, the major stockholder in Western Union and American gas utility companies. An even more significant new figure in the crowd of Edison backers was John Pierpont Morgan, the forty-two-year-old scion of a financial dynasty, and cofounding partner of the prestigious Drexel Morgan banking house, which later became J. P. Morgan and Company. Pierpont Morgan was hardly prone to speculative investments. He was, however, a director of Western Union and well acquainted with Lowrey, whose legal offices were in the same building as Drexel Morgan in New York, and whose early reports of Edison's lamp left Morgan imagining that something materially historic could come from it.

The Morgan seal of approval gave Edison precious advantages over his competitors, while a battery of Morgan partners also kept pressure on Edison to produce timely results. Morgan partners Egisto P. Fabbri and James Hood Wright became directors of Edison Electric Light Company, a firm organized in October 1878 to fund Edison's experiments, and the bankers formed the Edison Electric Illuminating Company of New York, the company that financed Edison's first permanent power station and distribution system. Morgan interests also promoted the exhibition of Edison's system abroad, protected his foreign patents, and founded Edison's electric light enterprises in England, then guided the corporate merger that eventually resolved patent disputes between Edison and Joseph Swan. Indeed, the first lights to be lit by Edison's pioneering central station in New York City were in the offices of Drexel Morgan, which had been outfitted with 106 lamps.

Groundbreaking for the world's first central power station and lighting distribution system had begun in 1881, in lower Manhattan, at the heart of the financial district and what was then the center of New York City's newspaper industry. The power station on Pearl Street was outfitted with six Jumbo dynamos, built nearby at the newly established Edison Machine Works. As Edison and his key research associates supervised construction and testing of the entire system, the center of the inventor's activities shifted away from Menlo Park. By September 4, 1882, when he opened the Pearl Street Station, the inventor had moved his lamp company to East Newark, and by November 1882 his Menlo Park laboratory was abandoned in favor of working quarters in Manhattan. His family moved to New York City as well, and the family by now consisted of his wife and three children: daughter Marion and sons Thomas Alva Jr. and William Leslie.

Edison unquestionably preferred the culture of his work to the pleasures of his family. In 1878, for instance, when the newspapers reported that he and Mary were expecting their third child, Edison was quoted as saying, "The phonograph is my baby," giving a good indication how work and family would compete for his attention, and which would win. Later that summer, evidently suffering from exhaustion as a result of his breakneck pace in developing and promoting the phonograph, the inventor left home for a long trip that combined research and professional engagements with a vacation. Mary stayed in Menlo Park, pregnant and ill with "nervous prostration," a condition for which there is no reliable medical definition today, yet was frequently the diagnosis for symptoms of depression, anxiety, and, where women were concerned, "hysteria." By the time William Edison was born in October, the inventor was completely preoccupied with electric lighting. Edison did take winter vacations with his family during 1882–84, and the rest was meant to benefit the health of himself and his wife, who continued to be plagued by idiopathic symptoms during these years. She died from unknown causes in August 1884. Edison did not stay widowed for long. By the following autumn, he proposed to Mina Miller, whom he married in February 1886.

The second marriage would bring another three children—Madeline was born in 1888, Charles in 1890, and Theodore in 1898—yet Edison's second marriage differed from his first in several respects. Mary Stilwell was strictly working class, a woman whom Edison had met when he was her employer as well as a struggling inventor; Mina

Miller was introduced to him through social rather than workplace connections, and she was the epitome of middle-class domesticity. The product of finishing school, and herself the daughter of an inventor and manufacturer of agricultural machinery from Akron, Ohio, she was also nearly twenty years younger than Edison, America's foremost inventor. Edison's second bride enjoyed many comforts her predecessor had not. She was given a mansion worth $235,000 in Llewellyn Park, an exclusive residential community in West Orange, New Jersey, and part of the couple's honeymoon took them to Florida, where Edison established a winter home in Fort Myers.

Soon after his second marriage, Edison revived his interest in establishing a central research facility, on a grander scale than Menlo Park. He purchased fourteen acres in West Orange, in the valley below his home, and proceeded to construct the most advanced laboratory complex of its kind. In 1887 he spent more than $140,000 on buildings and equipment. His library/office was an impressively spacious wood-paneled room, with an immense fireplace, arched windows, and two levels of open tiered galleries, rising above the ground level, and surrounding three of the four walls. The room could hold as many as 36,000 books. It was also the only conspicuously elegant portion of the laboratory complex. The rest of the facility boasted a different aesthetic, for it was strictly functional, although lavish in that regard, and replete with machinery and raw materials. A power plant supplied electricity for the 650 lamps within the different buildings, including a chemical laboratory, a laboratory for electromagnetic experimentation, a shop for making patterns, and a metallurgical laboratory. All together the laboratory complex soon employed as many as thirty experimenters and technical assistants, plus an additional labor force of machinists, pattern makers, draftsmen, carpenters, clerks, and others.

One of the most important research associates at Edison's new "invention factory" was William Kennedy Laurie Dickson. An engineer and amateur photographer, Dickson left his job at Edison's lamp factory to help improve Edison's phonographs and pioneer his development of motion pictures.

Edison's residence and laboratory in West Orange point out several themes concerning Edison and his era. It was an age of conspicuous consumption, when William K. Vanderbilt and his father built a pair of mansions on New York's Fifth Avenue, reportedly costing $15 million, yet most Americans lived very modestly. Annual incomes for 1890 ranged from $233 for farm laborers to $439 for manufacturing employ-

Edison's West Orange Laboratory Successor to Menlo Park, the West Orange laboratory institutionalized Edison's methods. The main building included Edison's library/office, as well as machine shops, drafting rooms, and a storeroom. Visible in the background are factories eventually built to manufacture inventions perfected at the lab.

ees, and from $687 for employees of gas and electrical utilities to $848 for clerical workers in manufacturing and steam railroad enterprises. Garment workers often worked eleven-hour shifts in crowded sweatshops for less than a dollar per day, while miners worked nearly as long for perhaps twice as much pay. Where Edison stood within this spectrum is not without interest. There were companies bearing Edison's name throughout the world, and his income was obviously nearer to that of a Vanderbilt than the average American, but Edison's visible display of wealth was modest among millionaires. He also had no interest in high society, he remained a mechanic at heart, and he worked days as long as any garment worker or miner.

By 1889 Edison had executed 652 patent applications with dozens more pending. His presence at the Paris Exposition of 1889 gave Americans as much pride in their nation as the French garnered from the opening of the Eiffel Tower. He had additionally formed the Edison General Electric Company, a move toward consolidating his lamp, dynamo, and lighting fixture companies into one enterprise. Edison had also entered a new phase of inventive activity, and in the years to come, though every so often he would announce his retirement, he never completely retired or quit.

In the next phase of Edison's inventing, he returned to developing phonographs, wanting to see "his baby" reach maturity after he noticed that the baby was falling behind the progeny of others. Alexander Graham Bell and Charles Sumner Tainter unveiled their "graphophone" in May 1887, the same month in which German American inventor Emile Berliner applied for a patent on his "gramophone." Not to be outdone, Edison soon revisited nearly every component in the design of his phonograph: the power supply, the recording material, the quality and volume of the sound, and the procedures for cheaply duplicating recordings. Phonographs (and graphophones) remained able to record as well as play back sound, and the most profitable application of such machines was expected to be their use as dictation devices for business correspondence. Additional uses remained conceivable but subsidiary, even though Edison had developed a "phonograph for dolls and other toys" by 1889. Further inventive contributions by Edison and others would soon help to reframe the phonograph as an amusement device that would play prerecorded musical records.

In addition, in 1888 Edison promised he would invent something to "do for the eye what the phonograph does for the ear." His interest in the nascent technology of motion pictures was stimulated by consultations with the world's two greatest experts in the science and technique of serialized action photography. One was photographer Eadweard Muybridge, whose visit with Edison in West Orange that year led the inventor to propose a device called the kinetoscope. The other direct influence on Edison was physiologist Étienne-Jules Marey, who took sequential photographs of moving figures by "shooting" them with a gun-like camera. In 1889 Edison made W. K. L. Dickson his key experimenter for motion pictures, and set him to work on various problems, thinking that photographic emulsion could attach images to a cylinder, and they could be played back like a phonograph. Edison himself spent the bulk of his time on other matters.

Mining and ore milling were capturing the greater amount of his attention during the 1890s. Edison turned much of his personal energies and considerable amounts of his financial wealth toward the problem of obtaining concentrations of iron from low-grade ores.

Undertaking a decade-long endeavor, which drew upon his patented processes of magnetic separation, it led him to experiments in mass production, while never making a profit. The better part of his venture capital came from the gradual sale of Edison's stockholdings in the General Electric Company, which was formed in April 1892, when J. P. Morgan engineered the merger of the Thomson-Houston Electric Company with the Edison General Electric. During the 1890s, Edison effectively lost all control of the industry that he had helped to start, even though the public never wavered in its association of Edison and electricity.

Moreover, the research staff at Edison's laboratory continued to develop new technical ideas for commercial exploitation. The joint work of W. K. L. Dickson and William Heise made significant advances in the development of motion pictures between October 1890 and May 1891, producing a sprocket-feed mechanism for film that was remarkably similar to a printing telegraph. They began making viewers and cameras, then experimental films, leading Edison to give a few public demonstrations of the new kinetoscope, a way of presenting motion pictures to one viewer at a time. When the first kinetoscope parlor opened in New York during mid-1894, customers looked down into a cabinet and watched very short, simple subjects through a peephole, paying a nickel for each view. In less than one year, Edison earned nearly $90,000 in profits from the sale of kinetoscopes and films.

Then, just as quickly, the fad faded. After Dickson quit Edison's employ in April 1895 and went to work for the rival American Mutoscope Company, the production of new Edison films came to a halt. The next major breakthrough did not emerge from Edison's staff. Thomas Armat and C. Francis Jenkins coinvented a way to project motion pictures on a screen, making it possible for many people to view films at the same time in auditoriums. Edison eventually pooled his camera patents with those of the Armat-Jenkins projector, and agreed to supply the films, as well as to lend his illustrious name to the projector, which was called the "Edison Vitascope." It was introduced to the public at Koster & Bial's Music Hall in New York City on April 23, 1896.

Edison's problems were far from over, however. The Lumiére brothers in France were making a sensation with their cinématographe, another form of projected motion pictures, which arrived stateside during the summer. British inventors William Friese-Greene and Robert William Paul were similarly active in developing the new medium. Dickson's motion pictures were meanwhile being released by the American Mutoscope Company, and playing vaudeville houses. At the same time, further renegades from Edison's invention factory formed an additional competitor, the International Film Company, and began selling pirated copies of Edison's films before entering into production for themselves.

Edison responded to the competition in several ways. He introduced a modified projector, calling it his own, and he turned to the courts in an attempt to restrain the unauthorized use of his patents and to validate the copyrights on films. He also tried to make more popular films. His team turned out exotic subjects geared to excite the interests of audiences—from vistas in foreign lands and New York street scenes, to heart-stopping thrill sequences and ribald comedies. Current events offered another avenue for production: Along with footage from the Spanish-American War, reenactments of the Boer War, and some of the last photographs of President William McKinley before he was assassinated were captured by Edison's filmmakers.

The release of *The Great Train Robbery* (1903) scored new success for the Edison Manufacturing Company's motion picture division, largely due to the innovative talents of Edwin S. Porter, its cameraman, who collaborated with George S. Fleming, an actor and scenic designer, in the artistic direction, story development, and editing of the film. They produced a suspenseful, Western crime-action story, a multiscene narrative, and one of the earliest films with a developed scenario. It was also the first blockbuster, a moment to prove that movies could find massive popularity, even if hitting upon commercial success proved hard to predict or duplicate in every film. As the new entertainment industry underwent rapid growth and attracted widespread competition during the first decade of the twentieth century, Edison struggled to keep his motion picture business viable. Fighting competition through patent litigation, he also looked to enhance the technology. He contracted experimental work with color photography, spending approximately $30,000 to find a process (for which he received a patent but which he never introduced commercially). He also devised a patented system for talking pictures that mechanically connected phonographs with cameras and projectors, but he never synchronized sound and image reliably enough for full-scale commercial exploitation. In addition, Edison's company manufactured equipment for home and amateur use. His business was also party to the Motion Pictures Patent Company, a business concern that tried to dominate theatrical film, until it was declared to be an unlawful monopoly by the federal government.

The phonograph industry was no less vigorous than motion pictures. During the 1890s Emile Berliner and others began retailing disc record systems as a successful alternative to Edison's cylinder record system. The gramophone's sound was not as good as that of Edison's machines, but the discs were easier to handle and store than cylinders. They were also made of a more durable, thermoplastic shellac material, and they could be mass produced more cheaply than cylinders. The alternative format quickly cornered a lion's share of the market, due not only to the advantages of mass production, but also to a few key marketing policies adopted by the Victor Talking Machine Company, which took over the gramophone interests in America. Concentrating on the uses of recorded sound in the home, it ignored the business and educational markets, which Edison continued to pursue. Victor also introduced one of the most successful trademarks of the twentieth century: the picture of a dog frozen in curiosity, his ear cocked slightly toward the amplifying horn of a record player, while listening to "his master's voice" (now owned by RCA; HMV stands for "his master's voice"). The name of the Victor record player, the "Victrola," became a colloquial term for all record players. Corn flakes, celluloid, and escalators are names with similar histories, just as the trademarked Xerox®, Kleenex®, and Coke® today are considered synonymous with photocopies, tissues, and colas.

For years after the Victrola's success, Edison remained committed to the cylinder format for phonograph records. In 1912 he finally conceded that the disc recording system was here to stay. He experimented intensely and brought out his own line of disc machines and recordings, while also continuing to serve the cylinder market well into the 1920s. Edison wrote advertising slogans and reviewed promotional materials for his phonograph business. He also listened to auditions and strongly expressed his opinions, holding sway over what was recorded, despite his increasing deafness.

To some extent, Edison's experiences in the motion picture and phonograph industries were typical of his entire career. Edison was confident that his brain could solve anything it wanted to solve, yet his inventive and commercial work repeatedly produced ambiguous results. Since no one project or idea was fully isolated from another in Edison's mind, the formation of the Edison Portland Cement Company in 1899 speaks more fully to the same point. After

the 1898 discovery of Minnesota's iron-rich reserves made Edison's
ore-concentration scheme pointless, he closed his ore-milling plant,
yet wasted no time in turning his understanding of continuous production techniques to the manufacture of Portland cement.

By the end of the nineteenth century, natural cement was being
succeeded by Portland cement, a compound of calcium, silica, alu-
mina, and iron that produced a better bonding agent in concrete.
When strengthened with steel reinforcements, concrete promised to
become the world's most adaptable building material. Edison's cement
plant went into production in November 1903; twenty-five years later
the uses of his cement corresponded to the diverse adaptability of concrete in modern construction, finding its way into bridges, tunnels,
and roadways, schools, department stores, and swimming pools, as
well as New York's Yankee Stadium in the Bronx. His technical contributions to the industry included improvements to machinery for
crushing and screening rock, along with a significant breakthrough
for the industry in 1909: his invention of a giant rotary kiln that
proved to be capable of processing the ground stone mixture at five
times the industry average with greater fuel efficiency. Edison also
designed a method of using poured cement concrete to make affordable, quickly fabricated houses. Although few of the Edison-poured
houses were built, his idea seemed to grasp emerging trends in urban
renewal, modern architecture, and the beginnings of suburbia.

Nothing occupied Edison more in the early years of the twentieth
century, though, than his electrochemical research with wet-cell storage batteries. The experimental work alone probably involved more
than 50,000 laboratory tests conducted under Edison's supervision.
One of his major goals was to produce a light, portable, quickly
chargeable battery to be used in moving vehicles. More than one-third
of the cars and trucks in America were electrically powered before
World War I, before gasoline-powered motors became the decided
standard. The task of moving vehicles, however, was not the only
application for Edison's storage batteries. They could also be used for
electrical power in country houses, in submarines, in trolleys, in ware-
house dollies, and in portable lighting fixtures. When used to power
lamps that were attached to the helmets of underground miners, Edison's battery-powered light was considered to be a significant advance
for the occupational safety of miners.

As Edison approached his sixty-fifth birthday, he took a stab at
updating, or modernizing, the organization of his various research and
commercial activities. He formed Thomas A. Edison, Incorporated, in

1911 to coordinate the exploitation of his patents, manufacturing enterprises, and marketing operations. It hardly freed him from the day-to-day management of the businesses, for Edison found it difficult to let go of it all, even though his team of support staff had long ago grown beyond the day-to-day control of any single individual. He remained an active researcher, focused on his existing business rather than new ones, and therefore supervised and conducted experiments on various subjects related to the disc phonograph, business dictation machines, talking motion pictures, and the design and acoustic engineering of recording studios, as well as his storage battery. Then, in 1914, Edison's phonograph business was among the first American firms to be seriously affected by the outbreak of war in Europe, because it was so dependent upon German suppliers for the phenol used in its manufacture of records. If Edison was no longer inventing new industries, he was quick to resolve the problem for his own enterprise. After working night and day to find a substitute, he put up plants to manufacture the chemical himself. Those same plants were soon producing other chemicals, including toluol (one of the "t's" in TNT), which he supplied to the British through J. P. Morgan and Company. When America entered the war, Edison was named chairman of the Naval Consulting Board, a blue-ribbon consortium of military, governmental, and industrial interests that foreshadowed the "military-industrial complex." Edison went to meetings, but otherwise busied himself with experimental methods for detecting enemy submarines.

War-related contracts made great earnings for Edison's businesses. His factories and laboratory accommodated as many as 11,000 workers by the end of hostilities. After that, tough times settled in. Edison abandoned his unprofitable motion pictures business, and, during the 1920s, the phonograph business stopped being his cash cow. Indeed, all of Edison's businesses suffered in the postwar recession, but the phonograph losses continued to mount dramatically after the national economy boomed. One important reason was Edison's stubbornness. Most of the competition had converted to electrical recording, while Edison clung to acoustic techniques. Radio was the next wave, and Edison refused to get involved with it. Sound and color motion pictures were nearer to full commercial introduction, yet Edison had abandoned their development as well. Also, instead of updating his technology, Edison cut the payroll, reduced advertising budgets, and trimmed contract fees to artists. By 1921 the workforce at West Orange was reduced to 2,000 employees. Edison was the last to admit that his hands-on control of the business could be detrimental to its research, development, manufacturing, and commercial operations. Although Charles Edison, the elder son from his second marriage, became president of Thomas A. Edison, Inc. in 1926, Edison did not finally retire from business until 1927. Thereafter Charles and his brother Theodore, a graduate of the Massachusetts Institute of Technology, managed to make some moves toward the latest radio-phonograph technology. Before they could release anything for a new electrically recorded catalog, the Edison phonograph business was bankrupt. Edison's entertainment-phonograph business was discontinued in 1929.

Edison spent his last years trying to develop a domestic supply of natural rubber for commercial use. A strategic material that had been difficult to obtain during and immediately following the war, rubber was critical to the business of Edison's friends, automobile manufacturer Henry Ford and tire manufacturer Harvey Firestone, who funded his rubber research, even as they both invested in rubber plantations abroad. The inventor put nine acres of land into cultivation near his home in Fort Myers, Florida, collecting more than 17,000 plants for testing; when Edison died in 1931, the results of his experiments were inconclusive.

NOT JUST AN IDEA

Recognizing inventors and inventing is a relatively modern pursuit. No one knows who invented the wheel, the plow, or the stirrup. No one knows precisely how or when bronze, paper, or gunpowder was first created. The invention of printing with movable type is readily ascribed to a fifteenth-century Rhinelander, Johannes Gutenberg, but most of the people familiarly known as inventors are men who lived after the first half of the eighteenth century, during or after the Industrial Revolution, men like James Watt of the steam engine (1769), Eli Whitney of the cotton gin (1793), and Samuel F. B. Morse of the first American electric telegraph (1844). Although it is frequently misleading, new machines of note historically get attributed to the work of single individuals at particular moments. Invention is understood as a form or expression of individualism, although such a focus tends to promote a simplistic, romantic understanding of technology. Technological change is more properly a social process than it is the result of isolated acts of creative genius.

In some respects invention is a national concern as well as a modern one. Schoolchildren in Britain, for example, often learn that Joseph Swan, not Thomas Edison, invented the incandescent light bulb, that William K. L. Dickson, not Edison, invented motion pictures. Schoolchildren in France learn that Charles Cros, not Edison, invented the phonograph, and that the brothers August and Louis Lumiére invented motion pictures.

While the fact that inventions are attributed to different people in different nations must arise in part from pure chauvinism, it also suggests that technological artifacts like light bulbs and movies may be too complex to have been invented whole, in a single, dramatic moment or by a single individual. Instead, many inventors often work on the same problem, at times secretively but at other times publishing their accomplishments in the form of patents or, like Edison, trumpeting them to the press. Many, perhaps most, innovations occur uncelebrated in the course of everyday life and labor. Many inventors can make crucial contributions to a single technology. Whoever is eventually considered the inventor depends upon a great many factors, usually including but never limited to being the first and only person to achieve a certain technological goal or result. Other factors include the social and economic advantages an inventor might possess, the legal dexterity of an inventor's patent lawyers, consumer interest, public relations, and the ongoing description of history by historians, educators, politicians, and others. The point is not so much that some histories of who invented what are incorrect (of course, some are); the point is rather that inventing is a cultural phenomenon as well as a technological one.

In many respects Thomas Edison is the person who invented inventing as historians now understand it. It can be argued that this is Edison's greatest single achievement, dwarfing all of his other innovations. Edison realized that inventing meant a lot more than just being the first person to have a good idea. While he promoted himself as the inventor of many things, he was able to marshal and even to institutionalize many of the activities and resources that inventing entails, all in the context of his own hard work and creativity. His laboratories at Menlo Park and then at West Orange were his "invention factories." They represent important points of transition, helping to locate technological innovation between the isolated tinkers and primitive workshops of the past and the more modern, corporate R&D labs of today.

Edison's Menlo Park and West Orange laboratories each had advantages of location, materials and equipment, and personnel. Both were located with easy access to New York City, the nation's pre-eminent financial center and its primary communications and transportation hub. Both sites possessed land for Edison's endeavors, railroad links, and available sources of labor (although Edison had to sponsor the first boardinghouse in Menlo Park in order to provide himself with a crew). Throughout his career Edison had a knack for hiring people who could do what he needed to get done. His staff always included a core group of machinists who could make anything he called for, draftsmen who could turn his sketches into working plans, and secretaries to handle correspondence and help with administration. He hired chemists, mathematicians, and other specialists as needed. When his electric light work called for glass bulbs, he hired glassblowers like Ludwig Boehm, an instrument maker trained in Germany. When his financial backers wanted assurance of his electrical innovations, he hired a young physics student named Francis Upton to do a search of all of the relevant literature. When litigation with another inventor swirled around his light bulb, he hired draftsman and inventor Lewis Latimer right out of the enemy camp (Hiram Maxim's United States Electric Lighting Company) to give himself an edge. His staff was hierarchical, with some associates sharing more responsibilities than others and having freer reign to innovate, usually along lines that Edison suggested or at least on projects he assigned to them. There were unavoidable personality conflicts. The list of sometimes disgruntled laboratory alumni is a distinguished one, including Nikola Tesla, Reginald Fessenden, and Frank Sprague, the inventors of alternating current motors, high-frequency radio, and electric traction, respectively. Edison had some close associates, like Charles Batchelor, with whom there were apparently no ego conflicts involved in collaborating on Edison's inventions. Yet for others the very act of collaboration seemed to mitigate Edison's claims as the inventor.

Like many in his generation, Edison wrongly believed the ethnic, racial, and gender stereotypes of his day, but he seems to have appreciated and rewarded the abilities of individuals as such and in some cases. Lewis Latimer was African American; Nikola Tesla was a Croat from Serbia; both Charles Batchelor and W. K. L. Dickson were Englishmen. Over the years his laboratory staff included Germans, Swedes, and Slavs. He occasionally hired Jews. He usually counted on employing Italian immigrants for any manual labor he required at mines and mills. Women had no place at Edison's laboratory (he said of his own first wife that she could not "invent worth a damn"). Many working-class women, however, did find employment over the years in Edison's manufacturing businesses doing specialized detail work, including hand-coloring motion picture films or assembling tiny phonographs to make talking dolls. Detail-oriented manual labor was thought suitable for women, and manufacturers of the period liked to hire them for such jobs, because they could pay them less than they paid men.

Providing himself as much as possible with the necessary staff, materials, financial backing, and legal advocates, Edison worked with relentless energy on projects he deemed "practical." Practicality meant anticipating consumer demand in an existing or potential market, inventing something that people could be convinced to buy. Edison's work was goal oriented, whether he was after a new, louder version of Bell's telephone, a cheaper way to process iron ore, a replacement for domestic gas lighting, or a way to exploit x-rays. With such a goal in mind, Edison proceeded to articulate a research plan, thinking of things to try and subsidiary projects to work on. His method was trial and error, but always within a larger context. He tried hundreds of materials in his telephone receiver to see which worked best. He tried thousands of different filaments in his incandescent lamp before discovering that carbonized paper worked best, and then that carbonized bamboo fiber worked even better. Sometimes he knew what material would work best, but he wanted to find a cheaper version. Cobalt and rubber were fine for use in his rechargeable battery, but not if he had to rely upon expensive imports of both commodities. Platinum was necessary in electric lamps, but how could he use the smallest amount possible of this precious metal? He knew to vary one thing at a time, try everything, and then go back and work on another variable. And he knew that an important part of such work was record keeping. He filled hundreds of notebooks with his research notes and drawings, and his staff filled several thousand more, carefully dating and frequently signing entries that might be helpful later, either in reorienting his research plans or in defending his priority to the Patent Office or the federal courts. In one interview he called his notebooks his "novels." Together with Edison's correspondence, published accounts, and existing artifacts, this vast collection of experimental notes offers a look into the process of inventing, into the ongoing definition and redefinition of the practical.

Edison proved adept at finding financial backing for his endeavors—over the course of his long, on-again-off-again relationship with Western Union, and particularly after he was famous, when he sought investors for his electric lighting project. Part of his method was pure confidence; he pronounced his imminent success to the newspapers and to anyone else who would listen. When his investors grew worried, he invited them to his laboratory for demonstrations, dinner, and a taste of his braggadocio. He could be a canny salesperson, and he knew the advantages of showmanship. Some of his first lighting installations illuminated the yachts, homes, and offices of Cornelius Vanderbilt, J. P. Morgan and other eminent capitalists and financiers. In some respects his confidence became a self-fulfilling prophecy. With the right financial backers Edison had both the money to proceed and the attention necessary to shape his destiny as the one to watch. When he did have inventions to exploit, he tended to favor privately held corporations in which he held most of the stock. He saw himself as an inventor, but he always wanted his own manufacturing enterprises to support further inventing. In cases when he did not do the manufacturing himself, he granted exclusive rights to other parties on the condition that he received specified royalty payments. He and the lawyers and executives who worked for him recognized the value of intellectual property rights—patents, copyrights, and trademarks[3]—as a means of controlling markets.

Like financing, legal strategy was a crucial element of Edison's success. He always had a lawyer and was involved with legal disputes over patent rights from the mid-1870s until his death. Patent infringement suits cut two ways; sometimes Edison sued someone else for infringing his own rights, and sometimes he himself was sued for selling something that another inventor thought was not Edison's to sell. All of this wrangling began in the official quarter of the United States Patent Office, established by act of Congress in 1790, where inventors have to convince the government that they have indeed invented

---

[3]Each of these is a different form of intellectual property authorized by federal law. Patents apply to inventions, copyrights apply to writings or other creative expressions, and trademarks apply to commercial marks like brand names. Edison patented the technology he invented, he sought copyrights for the films he produced, and he received a trademark on his own signature for use in promoting and labeling his manufactured goods. Of the three, patents are hardest to obtain. Federal agents called Patent Examiners evaluate an applicant's claims and assess the nature and extent of invention before they can grant a patent, an exclusive seventeen-year right (today it is twenty years) to exploit the invention in question. Patents balance rewards for inventors (in the form of exclusive rights) against benefits to the public (granting rights for only a limited term).

something new and useful. Edison would sometimes urge his lawyers to "claim the earth" or "claim the solar system" in regard to a particular invention. One federal judge, while deciding an important electric light case in Edison's favor, chided his lawyers about "the haste which has always seemed to characterize Mr. Edison's efforts to patent every improvement, real or imaginary, which he has made or hoped to make." Edison understandably wanted his legal rights to be as broad as possible in order to protect himself against competitors.

CONTEXTS FOR TECHNOLOGICAL CHANGE

Why do some inventions succeed and others fail? What affects the "fit" (or lack thereof) between what an inventor thinks is practical and what groups of consumers embrace? Related to these questions are broader questions of technological and social change. Does technology progress in a necessary sequence, from gas lighting to electric, for instance, or is technological development more idiosyncratic? Does society merely change in response to new technology, or are there social conditions that themselves shape the direction and the pace of technological change? One particularly interesting way to address questions like these is to take a look at "failed" inventions or inventions that succeeded in completely unanticipated ways. There are plenty of devices and technical processes that have worked without ever having been successful. Or is this just another way of saying that they really did not work? It depends upon how you define success and failure.

Inventions that fail to become popular can be hard to study for the simple reason that successful ones tend to dominate the historical record. What works tends to blind us to failures and false starts along the way, warping our sense of contingency (what might have been) and therefore of change. The present starts to look inevitable: Of course there are electric lights; of course we can record sound. Even little things about technology take on an air of inevitability: Of course English-speakers say "Hello" when they pick up the telephone; of course electric wall sockets have the shape and placement that they do. One of the challenges facing the historian is to undo this sense of the inevitable, to see the past on its own terms. Every such technological development turns out to have been the result of individual interests and unplanned negotiations between innovation and the social and economic conditions that existed at the time. Alexander Graham

Bell apparently wanted people to say "Ahoy!" when they picked up the phone, but Anglo-American culture ended up with "Hello" as a form of unthinking social consensus. Wall sockets went through many different forms and only gradually arrived at the standard we recognize. Record labels, dial tones, electric currents, and the sprocket holes along a strip of film: Each of these was shaped by a complex array of forces, social as well as technological.

Because of his immense public stature, Thomas Edison provides a convenient way to see into failed inventions in two ways. First, he was so well known that his own less than successful inventions received a lot of public notice. His iron-ore processing methods, his rechargeable battery for electric vehicles, and his poured concrete house all received international attention, yet none entirely lived up to the inventor's expectations. The iron-ore concentrating mill he built in western New Jersey had to be shut down when it could not compete with cheaper ore arriving from newly discovered iron deposits in Minnesota. His rechargeable battery eventually worked well, but the automobile industry had committed itself by then to gasoline and the internal combustion engine. The concrete house just did not catch on. In each case Edison had made an astute reading of some of the pertinent social and economic conditions—the burgeoning steel industry, the increase in private automobiles and company fleets, and the need for cheap suburban housing—but there were other conditions that he did not or could not take into account, like the structure of competition and the habits of consumers. The most generous way to put this might be that he was ahead of his time.

Even some of Edison's most successful inventions did not succeed in quite the manner he thought they would. He invented the phonograph, for instance, as a device for recording as well as playback. He thought it would make a revolutionary dictation device, to assist businesspeople and replace stenographers. It might be used to preserve the speeches of "our Washingtons, our Lincolns, [and] our Gladstones," he thought, never imagining that the primary function of the phonograph would eventually be to play prerecorded music. Only when consumer demand had reshaped or reframed the device did he recognize the phonograph as the amusement device it became. Then he made millions of dollars on musical phonographs and the records his company produced and manufactured.

The second manner in which Edison can offer a glimpse of failed inventions is also the result of his celebrity. Over the years he became a lightning rod for the schemes of others, and thousands of people wrote to him with questions or ideas of their own. Whether realistic proposals or kooky fantasies, the questions and ideas that ordinary people sent to the inventor over the years provide a glimpse of futures that never arrived. Like so many science fiction stories, the letters of such would-be inventors imagine a better future, yet they were undoubtedly sincere nonfiction. Reading these letters provides a sometimes poignant reminder that technological development always has its insiders and its outsiders, and it further prompts questions about the agents of technological change. After his concrete house idea was widely publicized, for instance, Edison received inquiries from across the United States and around the world. One woman wrote from a sod house in Oklahoma, seeking a better dwelling for her family. Others, like American steel magnate Henry Phipps and the Archduke Ferdinand from Bosnia-Herzegovina,[4] wrote hoping that they could provide housing reforms for others.

The history of technology needs to be sought in the documentary record, even in primary sources like unsolicited and "crank," "begging," or "idea" letters, as Edison and his staff referred to them. Machines themselves, even a sequence of outdated machines arranged chronologically in a museum, can only offer a tiny part of their own story. There are many sources of related documentary evidence. We have only to consider the numerous ways Edison himself used paper in order to understand the great variety and suggestiveness of the documents pertinent to the history of technology. He used paper to record his work, to collect the work of his employees, to communicate his wishes and ideas, to tag and wrap up mineral samples, and to keep his accounts. But he also burned bits of paper to try as carbon filaments in his incandescent light bulbs and used paper tapes and sheets to test and retest his printing telegraph devices, "electric pens," typewriters and mimeographs. And he did all of this within the larger context of unrelenting attention from the newspapers and unflagging self-promotion to the press. All of these uses of paper resulted in documents of one kind or another. Those that have survived offer evidence of Edison's activities and their contexts.

---

[4]A few of the Phipps letters are included in chapter 4. The assassination of Archduke Ferdinand in 1914 was the event that precipitated World War I.

A NOTE ABOUT THE TEXT

What cannot be adequately conveyed by the documents reproduced here is the sheer quantity of material available in one form or another on the subjects of Thomas Edison and modern America. Documents at the Edison National Historic Site archive, for instance, number five million or more. For every item included here, there are many, many alternatives that have not been included.

The documents reproduced in the first chapter introduce Thomas Edison as "An American Character." Included are seven different types of document: an autobiographical reminiscence, a diary entry, two personal letters, a business letter, an experimental notebook entry, a magazine interview, and a magazine article (this last almost certainly ghostwritten). Each document offers a different point of access to Edison's character and in particular to Edison's voice, since all are "by Edison" under different circumstances and for different purposes. Can the documents in chapter 1 be used together to locate a single, consistent Edison voice? What was he really like? What do documents like these indicate about the problems historians and biographers face when dealing with famous subjects?

The documents reproduced in the second chapter, "The Fantastic Phonograph," include one reminiscence and seven published accounts that illustrate the groundswell of public acclaim that Edison experienced in 1878, when he unveiled his "speaking machine." The published items are drawn from six different kinds of periodicals, including daily papers like the *New York Times* and monthly magazines like the *North American Review.* On one hand they demonstrate the difficulty in generalizing about the press, and on the other hand they suggest the way in which technological progress and the person of the inventor formed powerful points of orientation for American readers of the period. These documents are particularly useful in their celebration of supposed future uses for the phonograph, none of which include its eventual use as an amusement device for playing mass-produced, prerecorded music. How was the new medium of recorded sound understood, or misunderstood, relative to the old media of writing and print? Some writers made jokes at the expense of Edison and his machine. Are these merely another indicator of his celebrity, or might they hint at prevailing cultural anxieties about technology and other conditions of modern life?

The documents in the third chapter, "Electric Light and Power," include experimental notes, telegrams and other correspondence, some official testimony, published accounts, and promotional items. One point they make together is that technological innovation involves many sorts of power, not just electrical power. Much of the necessary power was financial, some of it was litigious, and not a little of it involved drawing the right team of experimenters, the right materials, and the right research together at Menlo Park into a coordinated effort. Successful implementation of electric lighting involved still more financial power but also required municipal power: for instance, city governments had to agree to let Edison's company dig up the streets to bury wires. Unlike the previous chapter, chapter 3 includes very few newspaper accounts, favoring documents that were generated in or for more private contexts. These documents offer a way to see the private workings of Edison's laboratory, as well as to judge the dynamic balance of privacy and publicity that his work always entailed. Judging from the documents in chapter 3, what, when, and how did the public learn of Edison's progress on electric lighting? How was the private, behind-the-scenes work at Menlo Park affected by real and potential publicity? Do the private and public accounts of invention agree with one another about how Edison's incandescent lamp succeeded?

Chapter 4 reproduces documents pertinent to "Modern Living," a much broader subject than the invention and public unveiling of the phonograph in 1878 or the development of electric lighting in 1878–85. Many of the items reproduced in this chapter document Edison's continued stature as an American celebrity. They offer a glimpse of projects he tackled after electric lighting and suggest ways in which his interests and those of American society as a whole coincided and diverged at different times and under different circumstances. In keeping with his early work on what are now called "information technologies," many of Edison's later projects can be classified either as media or as instruments of social organization or social control. The "fluoroscope" he invented to show x-ray images of the body was a new medium presenting a whole new form of information. His attention turned likewise to public transit and private vehicles, and then to improved housing for the working class. Meanwhile, a new entertainment industry emerged as such, and Edison's companies produced phonograph records and motion pictures that helped to create new publics, new audiences with new appetites for the latest hit and the newest release.

Documents in chapter 4 focus on the developments of the 1890s and the early twentieth century, from the so-called Gilded Age to the

Progressive Era. They offer ways to pursue the themes of the preceding chapters as well as to question the character of American modernization in these years. How was the American public defined and redefined by emerging technologies? How were those technologies themselves defined by the interests of American society at large? If modernization had a price, who were its winners and who were its losers? Are there specific ways in which the early twentieth century resembles the early twenty-first century?

The documents include published and previously unpublished items. Many are being published or republished as part of the work of the Thomas A. Edison Papers Project, an ongoing endeavor supported by Rutgers, The State University of New Jersey; the National Park Service; the Smithsonian Institution; and the New Jersey Historical Commission. Other unpublished items appear here in print for the first time. Unless otherwise noted, the previously unpublished items exist in manuscript as part of the archive of the Edison National Historic Site in West Orange, New Jersey, and appear courtesy of the U.S. Department of the Interior, the National Park Service. Among the previously published items, many of the newspaper clippings included here are also part of that archive, collected by "clipping services" during Edison's own lifetime, so that he would have a record of his exposure in the press. Spelling and punctuation have usually been modernized and obscure abbreviations silently expanded by the editors, although efforts have been made to retain Edison's manner and tone in documents by him. Ellipses in the text indicate omissions by the editors.

1

An American Character

Since his own lifetime, Thomas Edison has been paradoxically received as both typical and singular, a representative American yet one of a kind. The documents in this chapter offer an opportunity to plumb that paradox and to assess Edison's character. Who was he, and where did his complex public persona come from? The items included here are all authored "by Edison," though their variety points up the difficulty of holding to a single version of authorship and a single version of the inventor. Of course Edison presented himself differently to different audiences. He was more or less formal in his style as circumstances required, and he seems to have been more or less self-conscious about his own celebrity at different times. He drew on accepted modes of social expression when he wrote formally to his prospective father-in-law, but he contrived a more personal voice when he penned witty comments in a semipublic diary and anecdotes for his biography. Taken individually, these documents each point to a slightly different Edison. Are they all equally reliable as evidence? How can they be taken together—contradictions and all—as suggestive of Edison's character? Would the biographies of similarly famous historical figures all present similar challenges?

Edison's Early Years, as He Remembered Them

1908–1909

When three of his associates began to write his authorized biography, Edison wrote out seven different batches of autobiographical notes for them to use. This document strings together a continuous narrative from those fragmentary batches, giving Edison's early life in his own words.[1] Like the Autobiography *of Benjamin Franklin, Edison's autobiographical notes offer a revealing response to his own standing as a public character at the same time that they depend upon a tone of contrived familiarity and of comic self-regard. His notes construct a very specific attitude toward the merits of industriousness and individualism.*

After my father moved to Port Huron [Michigan], he engaged in lumbering, and also had a 10 acre field of very rich land which was used for truck gardening [growing produce for local sale]. After the field was ploughed, I, in conjunction with a German boy of about my age, did the planting. About eight acres were planted in sweet corn, the balance in radishes, onions, parsnips, and beets, etc.; I was very ambitious about this garden and worked very hard. My father had an old horse and wagon and with this we carried the vegetables to the town, which was 1½ miles distant and sold them from door to door. One year I remember turning in to my mother 600 dollars from the farm.

After a while I tired of this work as hoeing in a hot sun is unattractive. . . . Soon the Grand Trunk R.R. was extended from Toronto to Port Huron at the foot of the Lake Huron and thence to Detroit, at about the same time the war of the Rebellion broke out. By a great amount of persistence I got permission from my mother to go on the local train as a newsboy. The local train from Port Huron to Detroit, a distance of 63 miles, left at 7 A.M. and arrived again at Port Huron at 9 P.M. After being on the train for several months, I started two stores in Port Huron, one for periodicals and the other for vegetables, butter and berries in the season, these were attended by two boys, who shared in the profits. The periodical store I soon closed, as the boy in charge could not be trusted. The vegetable store I kept up for nearly a year. After the railroad had been opened a short time they put on an

[1]For transcriptions of these documents as individually composed, see Appendix One, Volume One in Reese V. Jenkins et al., eds., *The Papers of Thomas A. Edison* (Baltimore: Johns Hopkins University Press, 1989).

express which left Detroit in the morning and returned in the evening. I received permission to put a newsboy on this train. Connected with this train was a car, one part for baggage and the other part for U.S. mail, but for a long time it was not used. Every morning I had two large baskets of vegetables from the Detroit Market loaded in the mail car and sent to Port Huron where the German boy would take them to the store. They were much better than those grown locally and sold readily. I never was asked to pay freight and to this day cannot explain why, except that I was so small and industrious and the nerve to appropriate a U.S. mail car to do a free freight biz so monumental that it probably caused passivity. However, I kept this up for a long time and in addition bought butter from the farmers along the line and an immense amount of blackberries in the season; I bought wholesale and at a low price and permitted the wives of the engineers and train-men to have the benefit of the rebate.

After a while there was a daily immigrant train put on. This train generally had from seven to ten coaches filled always with Norwegians, all bound for Iowa and Minnesota. On these trains I employed a boy who sold bread, tobacco and stick candy.

As the war progressed the daily newspaper sales became very profitable and I gave up the vegetable store, etc. Finally when the battle of Pittsburgh Landing occurred (now called Shiloh) I commenced to neglect my regular business. On the day of this battle when I arrived at Detroit, the bulletin boards were surrounded with dense crowds and it was announced that there were 60 thousand killed and wounded and the result was uncertain. I knew that if the same excitement was attained at the various small towns along the road and especially at Port Huron that the sale of papers would be great. I then conceived the idea of telegraphing the news ahead, went to the operator in the depot and by giving him Harper's *Weekly* and some other papers for three months, he agreed to telegraph to all the stations the matter on the bulletin board. I hurriedly copied it and he sent it, requesting the agents [to display] it on the blackboard, used for stating the arrival and departure of trains. I decided that instead of the usual 100 papers that I could sell 1000, but not having sufficient money to purchase that number, I determined in my desperation to see the Editor himself and get credit.

The great paper at that time was the Detroit Free Press. I walked into the office marked Editorial and told a young man that I wanted to see the Editor on important business—important to me anyway. I was taken into an office where there were two men, and I stated what I had done about telegraphy and that I wanted 1000 papers, but only had money for 300 and I wanted credit. One of the men refused it, but the other told the first spokesman to let me have them. This man I afterwards learned was Wilbur F. Storey, who subsequently founded the Chicago *Times* and became celebrated in the newspaper world.

By the aid of another boy we lugged the papers to the train and started folding them. The first station, called Utica, was a small one where I generally sold two papers. I saw a crowd ahead on the platform, thought it some excursion, but the moment I landed there was a rush for me; then I realized that the telegraph was a great invention. I sold 35 papers; the next station [was] Mt. Clemens, now a watering place but then a place of about 1000 [people]. I usually sold 6 to 8 papers. I decided that if I found a corresponding crowd there that the only thing to do to correct my lack of judgement in not getting more papers was to raise the price from 5 cents to 10. The crowd was there and I raised the price; at the various towns there were corresponding crowds. It had been my practice at Port Huron to jump from the train at a point about ¼ mile from the station where the train generally slackened speed. I had drawn several loads of sand at this point to jump on and had become very expert. The little German boy with the horse met me at this point. When the wagon approached the outskirts of the town I was met by a large crowd. I then yelled "25 cents apiece, gentlemen, I haven't got enough to go around!" I sold all out and made what to me was an immense sum of money.

I started the next day to learn telegraphy and also printing. I started a newspaper which I printed on the train, printing it from a galley proof press, procuring the type from a junk dealer who had a lot nearly worn out.

I commenced to neglect my regular business until it got very low, although I managed to turn one dollar each day to my mother. The station agent at Mt. Clemens permitted me to sit in the Telegraph office and listen to the instrument; one day his little boy was playing on the track when a freight train came along, and I luckily came out just in time to pull him off the track; his mother saw the operation and fainted. This put me in the good graces of Mr. Mackenzie, the agent, and he took considerable pains to teach me. As I kept at it about 18 hours a day I soon became quite proficient. I then put up a telegraph line from the station to the village, a distance of 1 mile, and opened an office in a drug store, but the business was small and the operator at Port Huron, knowing my proficiency and who wanted to go into the U.S. [Military] Telegraph, where the pay was high, succeeded in convincing his brother-in-law (Mr. Walker) that I could fill the position all right. Mr. Walker had a jewelry store and had charge of the W.U. Tel. [Western Union Telegraph] office. As I was to be found at the office both day and night, sleeping there, I became quite valuable to Mr. Walker.

After working all day I worked at the office nights as well for the reason that press reports came over one of the wires until 3 A.M., and I would cut in and copy it as well as I could, to become more rapidly proficient; the goal of the rural telegraph operator was to be able to "take press" [to receive press reports, which came in very quickly]. Mr. Walker tried to get my father to apprentice me at 20 dollars per month, but they could not agree.

I then applied for a job on the Grand Trunk R.R. as a railway [telegraph] operator and was given a place nights at Stratford Junction, Canada. This night job suited me as I could have the whole day to myself. I had the faculty of sleeping in a chair any time for a few minutes at a time. I taught the night yardman my [telegraphic] call, so I would get ½ hour sleep now and then between trains and in case the station was called, the watchman would awaken me. One night I got an order to hold a freight train and I replied that I would. I rushed out to find the signalman, but before I could find him and get the signal set, the train [ran] past. I ran to the Telegraph Office and reported I couldn't hold her, she had run past. The reply was "Hell." The dispatcher, on the strength of my message that I would hold the train, had permitted another to leave the last station in the opposite direction. There was a lower station near the Junction where the day operator slept. I started for it on foot. The night was dark and I fell in a culvert and was knocked senseless.

However, the track was straight, the trains saw each other, and there was no collision. The next morning Mr. Carter, the station agent and myself were ordered to come at once to the main office in Toronto. We appeared before the General Superintendent, W.J. Spicer, who started in hauling Mr. Carter over the coals for permitting such a young boy to hold such a responsible position. Then he took me in hand and stated that I could be sent to Kingston State Prison, etc. Just at this point, three English swells came into the office. There was a great shaking of hands and joy all around. Feeling that this was a good time to be neglected I silently made for the door; down the stairs to the lower freight station, got into the caboose going on the next freight, the conductor who I knew, and kept secluded until I landed a boy free of fear in the U.S. of America.

Up to the time of taking up telegraphy, I had a chemical laboratory on the train. A freight car had been fitted up as a baggage car and one end partitioned off as a smoking compartment. It was only 8 feet long, had a table in the middle and two benches. There was no ventilation and everybody went into the baggage end to smoke, hence, I had it all to myself. George Pullman had a small shop in Detroit, working on his sleeping car and he made me a lot of wooden apparatus for my chemicals. After I had done my train work, I would make chemical experiments. One day a bottle containing a stock of phosphorus jarred off on the floor and set it on fire. The baggage master put it out, but the phosphorus wouldn't go out and he picked it up to throw it out and some got on his fingers, and every time he rubbed it, it exposed a fresh surface and that got on fire. Water wouldn't put it out. He got a bad burn and boxed my ears so severely that I got somewhat deaf thereafter.

This deafness has been of great advantage to me in various ways. When in a telegraph office I could only hear the instrument directly on the table at which I sat, and unlike the other operators, I was not bothered by the other instruments. Again, in experimenting on the telephone, I had to improve the transmitter so I could hear it. This made the telephone commercial, as the telephone receiver of Bell was too weak to be used as a transmitter commercially.

After leaving Stratford Junction, I got a position as an operator on the Lakeshore & Michigan Southern at Adrian [Michigan], in the Division Superintendent's office. As usual I took the night job which most operators disliked but which I preferred as it gave me more leisure to Experiment. . . . I then went to Toledo and got a job at Fort Wayne [Indiana] on the Pittsburgh Fort Wayne & Chicago Rail Road now leased to the [Pennsylvania Rail Road]. This was a day job and I did not like it. I then got a place in the Western Union office in Indianapolis. . . . While the position was a day position I (taking no interest in anything except the telegraph) came around every night and on an adjoining table to the regular press operator would copy press until about 1 AM and then go home. But it came in faster than I could write it down legibly. At this time I conceived the idea of taking two old Morse Registers which recorded the dots & dashes by indenting a continuous strip of paper (the indenting point being worked by a lever & magnet); I arranged these 2 instruments so I could receive the regular press signals at their regular rate & record the same on the strip of paper. Of course I could have read and copied the signals from the paper, but taking by sound was the ambition of all operators, the old

Registers being obsolete. [So] I arranged the second register so that [as] the strip [passed] through it the indentations were made to actuate a delicate double lever causing the Local circuit of a sounder or receiving instrument to be opened & closed corresponding exactly to the original signals. This it did with great perfection. When press was coming over the wires at the rate of 40 words per minute, the paper strip passing into the 2nd Register repeated these signals audibly on the sounder but at the rate of 25 or 30 words per minute according to the speed of the clockwork, which could be varied at pleasure.

By the aid of another day operator who was ambitious I got permission from the press man to put this in circuit, and together we took press for several nights, my companion keeping the apparatus in adjustment, & I copying. The regular press operator would go to the theater or take a sleep, only finishing the report after 1 A.M. Soon one of the newspapers complained of bad copy etc. towards the end of the report, i.e. from 1 A.M. till 3, and requested that the operator taking the report up to 1 A.M., which was ourselves, take it all as the copy was objectionable. This led to an investigation by the manager & the scheme was forbidden. Of course having more time I could make better copy than the regular operator.

Not liking Indianapolis I obtained a situation in the Western Union office in Cincinnati on a way wire, [still] as a "plug" operator. Operators were designated as 1st class operators & plug operators, the latter being inefficient & there was very little association socially between the two classes.

When I was an operator in Cincinnati working the Louisville wire nights for a time [in 1865, and] one night a man on the Pittsburgh wire yelled out: "D.I. cipher!" which meant that there was a cipher message [i.e., in code] from the War Department in Washington and that it was coming—and he yelled out "Louisville!" I started immediately to call up that place. It was just at the change of shift in the office. I could not get Louisville [on the wire] and the cipher message began to come. It was taken by the operator on the other table direct from the War Department. It was for General Thomas, at Nashville. I called for about 20 minutes and notified them that I could not get Louisville. I kept at it for about 15 minutes longer and notified them that there was still no answer in Louisville. They then notified the War Department that they could not get Louisville. Then we tried to get it by all kinds of round about ways, but in no case could anybody get them at that office. Soon a message came from the War Department to send immediately for the manager of the Cincinnati office. He was brought to the office and several messages were exchanged, the contents of which, of course, I did not know, but the matter appeared to be very serious as they were afraid of General Hood of the Confederate Army who was then attempting to march on Nashville; and it was very important that this cipher of about 1200 words or so should be got through immediately to General Thomas. I kept on calling up to 12 or 1 o'clock but no Louisville. About 1 o'clock the operator at the Indianapolis office got hold of an operator on a wire which ran from Indianapolis to Louisville along the railroad, who happened to come into his office. He arranged with this operator to get horses, and the message was sent through Indianapolis to this operator who had engaged horses to carry the dispatches to Louisville and find out the trouble, and get the dispatches through without delay to General Thomas. In those days the telegraph fraternity was rather demoralized, and discipline was very lax. It was found out a couple of days afterwards that there were three night operators at Louisville. One of them had gone over to Jeffersonville and had fallen off a horse and broken his leg and was in a hospital. By a remarkable coincidence another of the men had been stabbed in a keno room [a gambling parlor] and was also in hospital, while the third operator had gone to Cynthiana to see a man hung and had got left by the train!

[After the war, there] came to work at [the] Cincinnati office a man by the name of George R. Ellsworth. This man was the telegraph operator of Morgan, the Confederate Guerrilla General who gave so much trouble to the Union by raiding & capturing or destroying stores. Ellsworth tapped wires, read messages, & sent false ones, and did an immense amount of mischief generally by his superior ability as an operator. It is well known that one operator can recognize another by the way he makes his signals, and Ellsworth possessed the art of imitating his peculiarities & therefore easily deceived the Union operators. We soon became acquainted & he wanted me to invent a secret method of sending dispatches so an intermediate operator could not tap the wire & understand it. He said that if it could be accomplished he could sell it to the government & get a large amount of money. This suited me & I started in & succeeded in making such an instrument, which had the germ of the Quadruplex in it, afterwards invented by myself and now generally used throughout the world. This Quadruplex permitted the sending of 4 messages over one wire simultaneously. . . .

The reason I came to go to Boston [in 1868] was this: I had left Louisville the second time and went home to see my parents. After stopping at home for some time, I got restless and thought I would like to work in the East and knowing that a former operator named Adams, who had worked with me in the Cincinnati Office, was in Boston, wrote him that I wanted a job there. He wrote back that if I came on immediately he could get me in the W.U. office. I had [just] helped out the Grand Trunk R.R. Telegraph people by a new device when they lost one of the two submarine cables they had across the river, making the remaining cable act just as well for their purpose as if they had two. I thought I was entitled to a pass [for the train], which they conceded, and I started for Boston. . . .

On reaching Boston, I found my friend Adams and went over to the W.U. Office to see the manager. On entering the office, where there were perhaps 30 or 40 men, I noticed that they were dressed very neatly, which was very unusual in the offices in the West. I myself, at the time, had on a blue shirt and clothes not of the best, and somewhat wrinkled from the long journey. I was introduced to the Manager, Mr. Milliken, who I thought gave a start of surprise. Adams had told him I was an A1 man and had worked two or three years on associated press wire. After asking me to confirm Adams' statements, he asked when I could come to work. I said "Now." "Very well, come around 5:30 and I will leave instructions." I came at 5:30 P.M. and was introduced to the night manager, and told that I was to work N.Y. No. 1 wire. I was furnished with one of those cheap pens that the W.U. used to economize on and waited for business. I noticed considerable talk and laughter on the part of the other operators and surmised that it was at my expense, as my clothes certainly did not fit extreme Eastern civilization.

After waiting ½ hour my wire was switched over on a test table in the middle of the room and I was told to take a 1500-word special for the Boston Herald. The N.Y. operator started at a rapid gate, the sending perfect and the wire was good. After a few minutes his gait got very rapid and I noticed he was getting up to his limit. Turning my head I found nearly every operator in the office watching me from behind. I knew then they had put up a job to roast me, as they say. They had gotten Hutchinson, one of the lightning senders in the N.Y. office, to do it. Now I had experimented a long time to acquire rapid penmanship. I indulged in no flourishes and each letter was separate and not connected, as I found that there was a gain in time in not connecting the letters and also that rapidity was increased by writing very small; I had been used to forcing the writing in taking press through 8 sheets of manifold paper with an agate stylus [to make 8 copies at once], so writing with a pen was easy. I then started writing very small and I knew I could do 4 or 5 words per minute more than he could send. After about ¾ of the special, Hutchinson got nervous and commenced to abbreviate. As I had to write out in full I knew that soon I would have to break, so to save the day before this took place, I opened the key and said, "You seem to be tired, suppose you send a little with your other foot." This saved me. Hutchinson quit and the special was finished by the regular man.

After this I was all right with the other operators.

In the Boston office there were operators studying to enter Harvard; they were on nights. They paraded their knowledge rather freely and it was my delight to go up to the second-hand book stores on Cornhill and study up questions which I might spring on them when I got an occasion. We got our midnight lunch from an old Irishman, called the "Cake Man," who appeared regularly at 12 midnight. The office was on the ground floor and had, previous to occupation by the Telegraph Co., been a restaurant. It was literally loaded with cockroaches, who lived between the wall and the board running around the room at the floor. These were such a bother on my table that I pasted two strips of tinfoil on the wall at my desk connecting one piece to the positive pole of the big battery supplying current to the wires and the negative pole to the other strip. The cockroaches moving up on the wall would pass over the strips, and the moment they got their legs across both strips, there was a flash of light and the cockroach went into gas. This automatic electrocution device attracted so much attention and got a ½ column description in an evening paper, that the Manager made me stop it.

Satirical Remarks from Edison's Only Diary

1885

In 1885 Edison was a young widower with three young children. That summer he was courting Mina Miller, his future second wife. He and Madeline, his twelve-year-old daughter, took a vacation with friends in Massachusetts, where Mina was also a guest. During that vacation Edison and other members of the party kept diaries, probably intending to circulate them among themselves for fun. This document forms the beginning of Edison's diary, as he heads from New Jersey to New York, before going off to Massachusetts. How does it compare to his autobiographical notes (which he composed years later) in tone and form? Do the two documents have a similar point of view? What was Edison really like?

MENLO PARK, N.J.
SUNDAY, JULY 12, 1885

... Awakened at 8:15 A.M. Powerful itching of my head, lots of white dry dandruff. What is this d—mnable material. Perhaps it's the dust from the dry literary matter I've crowded into my noodle lately. It's nomadic, gets all over my coat, must read about it in the Encyclopedia. Smoking too much makes me nervous, must lasso my natural tendency to acquire such habits, holding heavy cigar constantly in my mouth has deformed my upper lip, it has a sort of Havana curl. Arose at 9 o'clock came down stairs expecting twas too late for breakfast, twasn't. Couldn't eat much, nerves of stomach too nicotinny. The roots of tobacco plants must go clear through to hell. Satan's principle agent Dyspepsia must have charge of this branch of the vegetable kingdom. It has just occurred to me that the brain may digest certain portions of food, say the ethereal part, as well as the stomach. Perhaps dandruff is the excreta of the mind—the quantity of this material being directly proportional to the amount of reading one indulges in. A book on German metaphysics would thus easily ruin a dress suit. . . .

Holzer is going to use the old laboratory for the purpose of hatching chickens artificially by an electric incubator. He is very enthusiastic, gave me full details. He is a very patient and careful experimenter, think he will succeed. Everything succeeded in that old laboratory. Just think, electricity employed to cheat a poor hen out of the pleasures of maternity. Machine born chickens. What is home without a mother. I suggested to H that he vaccinate his hens with chicken pox virus, then the eggs would have their embryo hereditarily inoculated & none of the chickens would have the disease. For economy's sake he could start with one hen and rooster. He being a scientific man with no farm experience, I explained the necessity of having a rooster. He saw the force of this suggestion at once. . . .

MENLO PARK, N.J.
JULY 13, 1885

Woke (is there such a word) at 6 o'clock, slipped down the declivity of unconsciousness again until 7. Arose and tried to shave with a razor so dull that every time I scraped my face it looked as if I was in the throes of *cholera morbus*. By shaving often I too [sic] a certain extent circumvent the diabolical malignity of these razors. If I could get my mind down to details perhaps could learn to sharpen it, but on the other hand I might cut myself. As I had to catch the 7:30 A.M. train for New York I hurried breakfast, crowded meat, potatoes, eggs, coffee, tandem down into the chemical room of my body. I've now got dyspepsia in that diabolical thing that [Thomas] Carlyle calls the stomach, rushed and caught train. Bought a *New York World* at Elizabeth for my mental breakfast. Among the million of perfected mortals on Manhattan island two of them took in their heads to cut their navel chord from mother earth and be born into a new world, while two other less developed citizens stopped two of the neighbors from living. The details of these two little incidents conveyed to my mind what beautiful creatures we live among, and how with the aid of the police, civilization so rapidly advances.

Went to New York via Desbrosses Street ferry, took [horse-drawn street] cars across town. Saw a woman get into car that was so tall and frightfully thin as well as dried up that my mechanical mind at once conceived the idea that it would be the proper thing to run a lancet into her arm and knee joints and insert automatic self feeding oil cups to diminish the creaking when she walked. Got off at Broadway, tried the experiment of walking two miles to our office 65 5th Ave. with idea it would alleviate my dyspeptic pains. It didn't. Went into Scribner & Sons on way up, saw about a thousand books I wanted right off. Mind No. 1 said why not buy a box full and send to Boston now. Mind No. 2 (acquired and worldly mind) gave a most withering mental glance at mind No. 1 and said, You fool, buy only two books, these you can carry without trouble and will last until you get to Boston. Buying in New York to send to Boston is like "carrying coals to Newcastle." Of course I took the advice of this earthy adviser. Bought Aldrich's *Story of a Bad Boy,* which is sponge cake kind of literature, very witty and charming, and a work on Goethe & Schiller by Boynsen, which is soggy literature, a little wit & anecdote in this style of literature would have the same effect as baking soda on bread, give pleasing results.

Waited one hour for the appearance of a lawyer who is to cross-examine me on events that occurred 11 years ago. Went on stand at 11:30. He handed me a piece of paper with some figures on it, not another mark, asked in a childlike voice if these were my figures, what they were about and what day 11 years ago I made them. This implied compliment to the splendor of my memory was at first so pleasing to my vanity that I tried every means to trap my memory into stating just what he wanted. But then I thought what good is a compliment from a 10-cent lawyer, and I waived back my recollection. A lawsuit is the suicide of Time. Got through at 3:30 P.M. Waded through a lot of accumulated correspondence mostly relating to other people's business.

Edison as Suitor

1885

Edison wrote to John V. Miller and Theodore Miller a few months before he married their elder sister, Mina, and he wrote to their father asking for Mina's hand in marriage. Like Edison's autobiographical notes and his aborted diary, letters like these offer a glimpse at the different ways in which Edison presented himself to others. The letter to John and Theodore Miller gives an idea of the inventor's sense of humor, while together the letters help demonstrate the range of Edison's relationships with boys and men. There is little evidence to suggest what Edison's relationships with women were like. (John V. Miller eventually worked for Edison when he grew up; Theodore was fatally wounded in the Spanish American War of 1898.)

John and Theo.
I send you by Express today an electric shocking coil which one of the boys in the laboratory made from old material. . . .
  The coil is *very powerful.* I tried it on a Dutch carpenter today and it knocked him down instantly but it didn't hurt him. This was when the rod was in the coil and with 2 cells of battery, so there is no danger from one cell. It will shock 25 persons joining hands, and make a cat knock off the plastering. I sent you on the 22nd a telescope, which shows the rings of Saturn, etc. It is not too large for land views, and I hope it will suit you. I also ordered Messrs. Bunnell & Co. to send you a pair of telegraph instruments with battery and wire so you can set up a complete telegraph line from one part of the house to the other and learn to telegraph. Hoping you will have a Merry Christmas and not watch me and Mina so closely when I come again. I am, with the most distinguished consideration yours truly,

TA Edison

Edison to Lewis Miller

CORNER AVE. B & 17TH ST.

NEW YORK, SEPTEMBER 30, 1885

Dear Sir,

Some months since, as you are aware, I was introduced to your daughter Miss Mina. The friendship which ensued became admiration as I began to appreciate her gentleness and grace of manner, and her beauty and strength of mind.

That admiration has on my part ripened into love, and I have asked her to become my wife. She has referred me to you, and our engagement needs but for its confirmation your consent.

I trust you will not accuse me of egotism when I say that my life and history and standing are so well known as to call for no statement concerning myself. My reputation is so far made that I recognize I must be judged by it for good or ill.

I need only add in conclusion that the step I have taken in asking your daughter to entrust her happiness into my keeping has been the result of mature deliberation and with the full appreciation of the responsibility I have assumed and the duty I have undertaken to fulfill.

I do not deny that your answer will seriously affect my happiness, and I trust my suit may meet with your approval.

Very sincerely yours,

Thomas A. Edison

The Site of Invention: Edison's Draft Letter to James Hood Wright

1887

As his new laboratory in West Orange, New Jersey, was taking shape, Edison approached one potential financial backer with a proposal to build "a great Industrial works." The proposal is rendered here as a draft letter that Edison wrote out in longhand in the pages of one of his experimental notebooks. In it he sketches the promise of his lab as a site for continual invention, a place where inventions can be made, and made to turn a profit. Nothing ever came of this specific proposal, but Edison put the general idea into practice. By 1910 Edison's West Orange laboratory quadrangle was hemmed in by factory buildings, which manufactured Edison phonographs, Edison storage batteries, and other Edison goods for sale.

Mr. Wright,

My laboratory will soon be completed. The dimensions are one building 250 ft. long, 50 wide & 3 stories; 4 other buildings 25 x 100, one story high, all of brick. I will have the best equipped & largest Laboratory extant, and the facilities incomparably superior to any other for rapid & cheap development of an invention, & working it up into Commercial shape with models, patterns, & special machinery. In fact, there is no similar institution in existence. We do our own castings [and] forging, can build anything from a lady's watch to a Locomotive.

The machine shop is sufficiently large to employ 50 men, & 30 men can be worked in the other parts of the works. Inventions that formerly took months & cost a large sum can now be done [in] 2 or 3 days with only very small expense, as I shall carry a stock of almost every conceivable material of every size and with the latest machinery. A man will produce 10 times as much as in a laboratory which has but little material, not of a size, [which spends] delays of days waiting for castings and machinery not universal or modern.

You are aware from your long acquaintance with me that I do not fly any financial kites, or speculate, and that the works which I control are well managed. In the early days of the shops it was necessary that I should largely manage them, 1st because the art had to be created, 2nd because I could get no men who were competent in such a new business; but as soon as it were possible, I put other persons in charge. I am perfectly well aware of the fact that my place is in the Laboratory, but I think you will admit that I know how a shop should be managed & also how to select men to manage them.

With this prelude, I will come to business: My ambition is to build up a great Industrial works in the Orange Valley starting in a small way & gradually working up. The Laboratory supplying the perfected inventions, models, patterns, & fitting up necessary special machinery in the factory for each invention. My plan contemplates to working of only that class of inventions which require but small investments for each and of a highly profitable nature & also of that character that the articles are only sold to Jobbers & Dealers, etc. No cumbersome inventions like the Electric Light. Such a works in time would be running on 30 or 40 special things of so diversified [a] nature that the average profit would scarcely ever be varied by competition, etc.

My plan is to form a Company with a large authorized Capital but all held in the treasury, to have a board of directors, etc. Having formed the Co. I bring before it say 5 or 6 small inventions; the board decides which ones they think will pay. Say 4 are selected. Estimates are made for bldg grounds & necessary machinery to start mfg these 4 inventions. Say 35,000; the cost of experimenting were say 5,000. The subscribers to the stock take 40,000 at par and give me 40,000 [worth] of stock. Thus of the profits ½ would go to the money & ½ to the inventor. But to insure the money: The money stock to have 5 percent preferential dividend, i.e. if the Co. earns only 5 percent the inventor gets nothing; if it earns 10 percent the inventor gets 5 & the money 5. If earnings are 20 percent the money of course gets 10 & Inventor 10. . . .

I honestly believe I can build up work in 15 or 20 years that will employ 10 to 15,000 persons & yield 500 percent to the pioneer stockholders. I propose starting with $30 @ 35,000 & 3 or 4 small inventions. Now Mr. Wright, do you think this practicable? If so, can you help me along with it?

—E.

A "Private Idea Book"

1888

The New Year, 1888, brought still more confident planning with regard to the new West Orange "invention factory." On January 3rd, Edison began a notebook he entitled "Private Idea Book," in which he listed items he planned to invent in the near future. The title Edison gave his notebook implies much about invention as it was and has been commonly regarded. The book was "private" because invention is supposedly a form of guarded self-expression or self-realization, of the private made successfully public, and it was an "idea" book because invention supposedly starts in the head, not in the hands or on top of a laboratory worktable: both suppositions deserve scrutiny. Ideas on Edison's list include machines and processes, adaptations and variations, as well as wholly new commodities. "Artificial silk" and "artificial ivory," for instance, might be considered particularly prescient descriptions of nylon and plas-

tic, neither of which existed at the time. But what could "ink for blind" possibly be?

THINGS DOING AND TO BE DONE.

Cotton picker
New standard phonograph
Hand turning phonograph
New slow speed cheap
   dynamo
New expansion pyromag-
   netic dynamo
Deaf apparatus
Electrical piano
Long distance telephone
   which employs devices
   of phonograph . . .
Motograph telephone
   [made] practical[2]
Artificial cable
Phonograph motor to work
   on 100 volt circuits
Duplicating [method for]
   phonograph cylinders
Deposits in vacu[um] on
   lace, gold & silver
Also on cotton molten com-
   pound of lustrous sur-
   face [to] imitate silk
Magnetic [ore] separator,
   large machine
Locking [or briquetting]
   material for iron sand
Artificial silk
Inflammable insulating
   material
Good wax for phonograms

Phonographic clocks
Large phonograph for
   novels . . .
Drawing fine wire
Toy phonograph for dolls . . .
Snow compressor
Glass plate water ore separa-
   tor
Tinned faced iron for stove
   castings
Refining copper
   electrically . . .
Platinum wire ice cutting
   machine
Silver wire wood cutting
   system
Silvering or coppering bolting
   cloth in vacu[um] for
   durability
Expansion mirror platinum-
   iridium wire in vacu[um]
Photograph through opaque
   screens
Boron filament
Hg [i.e., mercury] out of
   lamp
Artificial mother pearl
Red lead pencils equal to
   graphite
India ink
Tracing cloth
Ink for blind . . .

[2]The motograph was a telephone component that Edison invented and adapted throughout his career for various purposes.

Straightening alternating
current...
Miners' battery & lamp
Butter direct from milk...
Soften ink of books transfer
to copper plate & plate
to matrix
Telephone repeater

Substitute for hard rubber
Artificial ivory
Soften vegetable ivory to
press on sheets
Various batteries...
Marine telegraphy...
Siren phonograph...
Disk phonograph

Theodore Dreiser Interviews Edison for Success *Magazine*

1898

An Edison mystique arose from interviews such as this one, granted to the novelist Theodore Dreiser. These same anecdotes became well worn: Dreiser's discovery of a "workman" who turns out to be the inventor; Edison's own quips about his first patent, his sleep habits and methods. They were chestnuts that appeared time and again in the press, helping to construct the category of "inventors" and "inventing" in the mind of the public. In this interview Dreiser seems particularly interested in matters of compulsion or instinct, in what makes Edison tick.

To discover the opinion of Thomas A. Edison, concerning what makes and constitutes success in life is an easy matter, if one can only discover Mr. Edison. I camped three weeks in the vicinity of Orange, N.J., awaiting the opportunity to come upon the great inventor and voice my questions. It seemed a rather hopeless and discouraging affair until he was really before me; but, truth to say, he is one of the most accessible of men, and only reluctantly allows himself to be hedged in by the pressure of endless affairs. "Mr. Edison is always glad to see any visitor," said a gentleman who is continually with him, "except when he is hot on the trail of something he has been working for, and then it is as much as a man's head is worth to come in on him." He certainly was not hot on the trail of anything on the morning when, for seemingly the tenth time, I rang at the gate in the fence which surrounds the laboratory on Valley Road, Orange. A young man appeared, who conducted me up the walk to the elegant office and library of the great laboratory. It is a place, this library, not to be passed through without thought, for with a further store of volumes in his home, it contains one of the most costly and well-equipped scientific libraries in the world; the collection of writings on patent laws and patents, for instance, is absolutely exhaustive. It gives, at a glance, an idea of the breadth of the thought and sympathy of this man who grew up with scarcely a common school education.

On the second floor, in one of the offices of the machine-shop, I was asked to wait, while a grimy youth disappeared with my card, which he said he would "slip under the door of Mr. Edison's office." "Curious," I thought; "what a lord this man must be if they dare not even knock at his door!"

Thinking of this and gazing out the window, I waited until a workingman, who had entered softly, came up beside me. He looked with a sort of "Well, what is it?" in his eyes, and quickly it began to come to me that the man in the sooty, oil-stained clothes was Edison himself. The working garb seemed rather incongruous, but there was no mistaking the broad forehead, with its shock of blackish hair streaked with gray. The gray eyes, too, were revelations in the way of alert comprehensiveness.

"Oh!" was all I could get out at the time.

"Want to see me?" he said, smiling in the most youthful and genial way.

"Why,—yes, certainly, to be sure," I stammered.

He looked at me blankly.

"You'll have to talk louder," said an assistant who worked in another portion of the room; "He don't hear well."

This fact was new to me, but I raised my voice with celerity and piped thereafter in an exceedingly shrill key. After the usual humdrum opening remarks, in which he acknowledged with extreme good nature his age as fifty-two years, and that he was born in Erie County, O[hio,] of Dutch parentage, the family having emigrated to America in 1730, the particulars began to grow more interesting. . . .

"Had you patented many things up to the time of your coming East?" I queried.

"Nothing," said the inventor, ruminatively. "I received my first patent in 1869."

"For what?"

"A machine for recording votes and designed to be used in the State Legislature."

"I didn't know such machines were in use," I ventured.

"They ar'n't," he answered, with a merry twinkle. "The better it worked the more impossible it was; the sacred right of the minority, you know,—couldn't filibuster if they used it,—didn't use it."

"Oh!"

"Yes, it was an ingenious thing. Votes were clearly pointed and shown on a roll of paper, by a small machine attached to the desk of each member. I was made to learn that such an innovation was out of the question, but it taught me something."

"And that was?"

"To be sure of the practical need of, and demand for, a machine, before expending time and energy on it."

"Is that one of your maxims of success?"

"It is."

In this same year, Edison came from Boston to New York, friendless and in debt on account of the expenses of his experiment. For several weeks he wandered about town with actual hunger staring him in the face. It was a time of great financial excitement, and with that strange quality of Fortunism, which seems to be his chief characteristic, he entered the establishment of the Law Gold Reporting Company just as their entire plant had shut down on account of an accident in the machinery that could not be located. The heads of the firm were anxious and excited to the last degree, and a crowd of the Wall Street fraternity waited about for news which came not. The shabby stranger put his finger on the difficulty at once, and was given lucrative employment. In the rush of the metropolis, a man finds his true level without delay, especially when his talents are of so practical and brilliant a nature as were this young telegrapher's. It would be an absurdity to imagine an Edison hidden in New York. Within a short time, he was presented with a check for $40,000, as his share of a single invention—an improved stock printer. From this time, a national reputation was assured him. He was, too, now engaged upon the duplex and quadruplex systems—systems for sending two and four messages at the same time over a single wire,—which were to inaugurate almost a new era in telegraphy.

Recalling the incident of the Law Gold Reporting Company, I inquired: "Do you believe want urges a man to greater efforts and so to greater success?"

"It certainly makes him keep a sharp lookout. I think it does push a man along."

"Do you believe invention is a gift, or an acquired ability?"

"I think it's born in a man."

"And don't you believe that familiarity with certain mechanical conditions and defects naturally suggests improvements to any one?"

"No. Some people may be perfectly familiar with a machine all their days, knowing it inefficient, and never see a way to improve it."

"What do you think is the first requisite for success in your field, or any other?"

"The ability to apply your physical and mental energies to one problem incessantly without growing weary."

"Do you have regular hours, Mr. Edison?" I asked.

"Oh," he said, "I do not work hard now. I come to the laboratory about eight o'clock every day and go home to tea at six, and then I study for work on some problem until eleven, which is my hour for bed."

"Fourteen or fifteen hours a day can scarcely be called loafing," I suggested.

"Well," he replied, "for fourteen years I have worked on an average of twenty hours a day."

This astonishing brain has been known to puzzle itself for sixty consecutive hours over a refractory problem, its owner dropping quietly off into a long sleep when the job was done, to awake perfectly refreshed and ready for another siege. Mr. Dickson, a neighbor and familiar, gives an anecdote told by Edison which well illustrates his untiring energy and phenomenal endurance. In describing his Boston experience, Edison said he bought [the physicist Michael] Faraday's works on electricity, commenced to read them at three o'clock in the morning and continued until his room-mate arose, when they started on their long walk to get breakfast. That object was completely subordinated in Edison's mind to Faraday, and he suddenly remarked to his friend, "'Adams, I have got so much to do, and life is so short, that I have got to hustle,' and with that I started off on a dead run for my breakfast."

"Are your discoveries often brilliant intuitions? Do they come to you while you are lying awake at night?" I asked him.

"I never did anything worth doing by accident," he replied, "nor did any of my inventions come indirectly through accident, except the phonograph. No, when I have fully decided that a result is worth getting, I go about it, and make trial after trial, until it comes."

"I have always kept," continued Mr. Edison, "strictly within the lines of commercially useful inventions. I have never had any time to put on electrical wonders, valuable only as novelties to catch the popular fancy."

"What makes you work?" I asked with real curiosity. "What impels you to this constant, tireless struggle? You have shown that you care comparatively nothing for the money it makes you, and you have no particular enthusiasm for the attending fame. What is it!"

"I like it," he answered, after a moment of puzzled expression. "I don't know any other reason. Anything I have begun is always on my mind, and I am not easy while away from it, until it is finished; and then I hate it."

"Hate it?" I said.

"Yes," he affirmed, "when it is all done and is a success, I can't bear the sight of it. I haven't used a telephone in ten years, and I would go out of my way any day to miss an incandescent light."

"You lay down rather severe rules for one who wishes to succeed in life," I ventured, "working eighteen hours a day."

"Not at all," he said. "You do something all day long, don't you? Everyone does. If you get up at seven o'clock and go to bed at eleven, you have put in sixteen good hours, and it is certain with most men, that they have been doing something all the time. They have been either walking, or reading, or writing, or thinking. The only trouble is that they do it about a great many things and I do it about one. If they took the time in question and applied it in one direction, to one object, they would succeed. Success is sure to follow such application. The trouble lies in the fact that people do not have an object—one thing to which they stick, letting all else go."

"You believe, of course," I suggested, "that much remains to be discovered in the realm of electricity?"

"It is the field of fields," he answered. "We can't talk of that, but it holds the secrets which will reorganize the life of the world."

"You have discovered much about it," I said, smiling.

"Yes," he said, "and yet very little in comparison with the possibilities that appear."

"How many inventions have you patented?"

"Only six hundred," he answered, "but I have made application for some three hundred more."

"And do you expect to retire soon, after all this?"

"I hope not," he said, almost parenthetically. "I hope I will be able to work right on to the close. I shouldn't care to loaf."

Shouldn't care to loaf! What a thought after fifty-two years of such magnificent achievement.

"The Tomorrows of Electricity and Invention"
by Thomas A. Edison
1910

In articles like this one from the magazine Popular Electricity in Plain English *(June 1910), Edison kept his name alive as a popular spokesperson for progress. This example contains some liberal thinking about cooperative economic structures as well as some idiosyncratic—and characteristically Edisonian—comments on diet. It touches upon contemporary concerns as wide-ranging as transportation, suburbanization, and economic growth, while it dissimulates the degree to which technology had become the work of experts, of engineers, rather than of amateurs and self-taught, self-made men.*

I understand that the readers of Popular Electricity are numbered among those who are interested rather in the future of electricity than its past. I shall be glad to be counted as belonging to this class, for while no longer young in the sense of mere years, it is with what electricity can yet do that I am concerned in these days. If I thought that the possibilities of electrical development were exhausted I should not give it a moment's consideration. Sometimes fathers come to me, or write to me, about their sons, and want to know if in view of the fact that so much of the field of work is already occupied by electricity, I would recommend it as a career. It is assumed by them that all the great electrical inventions have been made, and that nine or ten billions of dollars is about all that electricity will stand, in the way of investment. Well, if I were beginning my own career again, I should ask no better field in which to work. The changes for big, new electrical inventions are much greater than before the telegraph, the telephone, the electric light and the electric motor were invented; while each of these things is far from perfect. We shall have easily $50,000,000,000 of money in electrical services in 1925, and five times as many persons will then be employed in electricity as now, most of them in branches for which we have not yet got even a name. I often pick up my laboratory notebooks, of which I have hundreds, full of hints and suggestions and peeps into Nature, and realize how little we have actually done to set electricity at work, let alone determine its secret. Why, barely thirty years ago there was no dynamo in the world capable of supplying current cheaply and efficiently to the little incandescent lamp, and some of the keenest thinkers of the time doubted if the subdivision of the electric light was possible. [The British scientist John] Tyndall remarked in a public lecture, with a dubious shake of his head, that he would rather Mr. Edison should have the job than himself. It is those that will work at the art in the next fifty years that are to be envied. We poor gropers of the last fifty are like the struggling farmers among the bare New England rocks before the wide grain fields of the West were reached. The crops have been thin, without reapers or threshers to harvest them. We haven't gotten very far, yet, beyond [Benjamin] Franklin or [Michael] Faraday.

Look at the simple chances of improvement in what devices are known today. They are endless. . . . We must break new ground. . . . I am ashamed at the number of things around my house and shops that are done by animals—human beings, I mean—and ought to be done by a motor without any sense of fatigue or pain. Hereafter a motor must do all the chores.

Just the same remarks apply outdoors. For the past years I have been trying to perfect a storage battery and have now rendered it entirely suitable to automobile and other work. There is absolutely no reason why horses should be allowed within city limits, for between the gasoline and the electric car, no room is left for them. They are not needed. The cow and the pig have gone, and the horse is still more undesirable. A higher public idea of health and cleanliness is working toward such a banishment very swiftly, and then we shall have decent streets made out of strips of cobblestones bordered by sidewalks. The worst use of money is to make a fine thoroughfare and then turn it over to horses. Besides that, the change will put humane societies out of business. Many people now charge their own batteries because of lack of facilities; but I believe central stations will find this work very soon the largest part of their load. The New York Edison Company or the Chicago Edison should have as much current going out for storage batteries in automobiles and trucks as for power motors, and it will be so some near day. A central station plant ought to be busy twenty-four hours. It doesn't have to sleep. So far, we electrical engineers have given our attention to two-thirds of the clock; and between 10 P.M. and 6 A.M. have practically put up our shutters, like a retail store. I am proposing to fill up that idle part of the clock.

Electricity is the only thing I know that has become cheaper in the last ten years, and such work as I have indicated, tending to its universal use from one common source, is all aimed consciously or insensibly in that direction. I have been deeply impressed with the agitation and talk about the higher cost of living, and find my thoughts incessantly turning in that direction. Prices are staggering! Before I became a newsboy on the Grand Trunk Railroad, I raised and distributed market garden "sass" grown at the old home at Port Huron, Michigan, and made many a dollar for my crude little experiments that my mother with great doubt and trepidation let me carry on. Thus with early experience as a grower and distributor, reinforced by fifty years of inventing and manufacturing, I am convinced pretty firmly that a large part of our heightened expense of living comes from the cost of delivering small quantities to the "ultimate consumer."

My poor neighbors in Orange pay four or five times what I do for a ton of coal because they buy in such small quantities; and thus the burden falls on the wrong shoulders. This appeals to my selfishness as well as to my philanthropy, for the workingman hasn't much left to buy my phonograph or to see my moving pictures with, if all he makes is swallowed up in rent, clothing, and food. I'll speak about rent a little later. In clothing we have got onto the universal "ready-made" basis which has vastly cheapened dress while ensuring a fastidious fit. When we come to food let us note how far we have already gone in centralizing production of the "package[d goods]." I believe that a family could live the year round without using anything but good "package" food. What is needed is to carry that a step further and devise automatic stores where the distributing cost is brought down to a minimum on every article handled. A few electro-magnets controlling chutes and hoppers, and the thing is done. I wonder [that] the big five-and-ten cent stores don't try the thing out, so that even a small package of coal or potatoes would cost the poor man relatively no more than if he took a carload. If I get the time I hope to produce a vending machine and store that will deliver specific quantities of supplies as paid for, on the spot.

Butchers' meat is one of the elements in high cost of living that this plan may not apply to readily; but it is amazing how far, even now, automatic machinery goes in carving up a carcass. We shall simply have to push those processes a little further. Thousands of motors are now in use running sausage machines, for example. Besides, I am not particularly anxious to help people eat more meat. I would rather help them eat less. Meat eating like sleeping is a bad habit to indulge. The death rate and sickness of the population of the country could be reduced several percent, in the ratio of abstinence from animal food.

One most important item in the modern high cost of living is rent. The electric railway has been an enormous factor for good in distributing people so as to lessen congestion and lower rents. But homes and rents are still much too high in price because of the cost of construction. I saw it coming long ago and hence went into the making of cement, the cheapest and most durable building material man has ever had. Wood will rot and burn, but a cement and iron structure seems to last forever. Look at the old Roman baths. Their walls are as solid today as when built two thousand years ago.

2

The Fantastic Phonograph

By the autumn of 1877 Edison and his work on telegraphy were both relatively well known within a narrow circle of business leaders, scientists, and inventors who themselves worked on telegraphs of various kinds. These telegraphs included Alexander Graham Bell's telephone, recently unveiled to the public at the Centennial Exposition in Philadelphia in 1876. Because it was so new and strange, it was helpful to describe Bell's invention in terms of something old. For this reason Edison and his circle sometimes thought of telephones as "speaking telegraphs" to begin with. They were telegraphs you could speak through. While working on telegraphs and speaking telegraphs, Edison invented his own "speaking phonograph" that autumn, and for the first time it became possible to record sound for later playback. Announcements in the press and a host of public demonstrations made Edison world famous within a matter of months.

This chapter begins with a reminiscence by one of Edison's assistants and then presents a variety of press accounts from amid the bubble of attention Edison and his phonograph received in 1878. Although very different in tone and provenance, one thing that all of these accounts make clear is that no one yet understood what a phonograph really was. Or, to put that another way, no one in 1878 could know that phonographs would eventually be used to play prerecorded musical albums as part of an entertainment industry and within a trajectory that would lead to commodities like cassette tapes, CDs, and MP3 files.

Invention of the Phonograph,
as Recalled by Edison's Assistant,
by Charles Batchelor

ca. 1906

This document helps locate Edison's invention of the phonograph within the workings of his Menlo Park laboratory, where he and his staff were bent on making valuable improvements to different telegraph devices and to Alexander Graham Bell's telephone, here improved into what they called "Edison's Carbon telephone." As Edison's assistant Charles Batchelor remembered it many years after the fact, the phonograph was both the logical outcome of ongoing work at the laboratory and a stunning surprise. He describes the invention of 1877 as at once "brilliant" and "obvious." What does he mean?

This occurred at Menlo Park, N.J., in the Edison Laboratory, about the middle of the month of November 1877. I was Mr. Edison's chief assistant at that time and had been so for some years. We had been at work off & on for years previous to this time and had developed a system of automatic telegraphy, one of the instruments for which consisted of a rapidly running small wheel carrying forward a strip of paper, with a stylus resting on it to record chemically the dots & dashes that came over the line. Some of these instruments we had in the laboratory & much of the paper. We had also for a long time been developing the "Edison Carbon telephone," an instrument in which a diaphragm was made to put a varying pressure upon a button of pressed carbon by the vibrations produced by the human voice. Many of these instruments were in the laboratory at the time and we used them daily. Some years previous to this date we had designed and made some machines for coating paper with paraffin (similar to the [waxed] paper now used to wrap candy in) for making condensers for electrical work and a large lot of variable thicknesses of this paper, coated and uncoated, was stocked away in the cupboards.

When making different size telephone diaphragms it was a very common usage to mount them in a frame with a mouthpiece, hold them up, and talk to them in a loud or low voice; at the same time putting a finder close to the center to feel how much vibration was communicated to them.

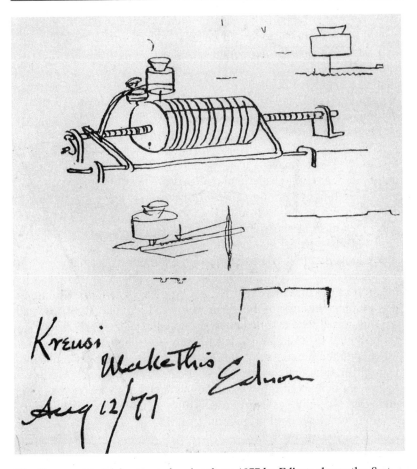

The Phonograph A laboratory drawing from 1877 by Edison shows the first phonograph and directs his machinist to "make this."
Courtesy of the Edison National Historic Site, National Park Service, U.S. Department of the Interior.

One night, after supper (which was prepared for us at midnight), at which all the principal workers sat down together, Mr. Edison who had been trying different diaphragms in this matter, suddenly remarked, "Do you know Batch, I believe if we put a point on the center of that diaphragm and talked to it whilst we pulled some of that waxed paper under it so that it could indent it, it would give us back talking when we pulled the paper through a second time." The brilliance of the suggestion did not at first strike any of us. It was so obvious that it would do so that everyone said "Why of course it must!"

I said, "We'll try it mighty quick," and we went to work. Mr. Kruesi the Chief Mechanician took the diaphragm to solder on to it at the middle a needle point about ¼″ long; he also took one of the automatic telegraph wheels and stands to fasten the diaphragm to so that we could draw the paper through easily.

I cut and got ready some strips of paper of different thicknesses of paraffin coating. It was a matter of an hour or so when we all got together again to make a trial. We fixed the instrument onto a table and I put in a strip of paper and adjusted the needle point down until it just pressed lightly on the paper. Mr. Edison sat down and putting his mouth to the mouthpiece delivered one of our favorite stereotyped sentences used in experimenting on the telephone, "Mary had a little lamb," whilst I pulled the paper through.

We looked at the strip and noticed the irregular marks; then we put it in again and I pulled it through as nearly at the same speed as I had pulled it in the first place and we got "ary ad elll am," something that was not fine talking, but the shape of it was there and so like the talking that we all let out a yell of satisfaction and a "Golly it's there!" and shook hands all round. We tried it many times and in many different ways continually improving the apparatus during the early morning. During the time that some of these changes were being made Edison & I would talk about the possibilities of such an invention, and it was then that we fully realized the brilliancy of the suggestion and the magnitude of the possible applications. . . .

The Phonograph Causes a Stir

March–June 1878

These documents capture something of the breadth of exposure Edison and his invention received in 1878. Items such as these eventually appeared in many different kinds of periodicals across the United States and abroad. Newspapers reprinted one another, recirculating excerpts drawn from quarterlies, weeklies, and dailies, while they also published their own editorial remarks and accounts of local phonograph demonstrations. Some writers were incredulous, most were adulatory, a few poked fun. Together they offer a way to think about the relatively chaotic ways in which new media emerge into public consciousness.

New York Times, **March 25, 1878**

Something ought to be done to Mr. Edison, and there is a growing conviction that it had better be done with a hemp rope. Mr. Edison has invented too many things, and almost without exception they are things of the most deleterious character. He has been addicted to electricity for many years, and it is not very long ago that he became notorious for having discovered a new force, though he has since kept it carefully concealed, either upon his person or elsewhere. Recently he invented the phonograph, a machine that catches the lightest whisper of conversation and stores it up, so that at any future time it can be brought out, to the confusion of the original speaker. This machine will eventually destroy all confidence between man and man, and render more dangerous than ever woman's want of confidence in woman.

New York Times, **April 20, 1878**

THE EDISON SPEAKING MACHINE.

EXHIBITION BEFORE MEMBERS OF CONGRESS—
THE PRACTICAL USES TO WHICH IT MAY BE APPLIED.

WASHINGTON, April 19.
Mr. Edison, the inventor of the phonograph, gave exhibitions with the instrument today at the Capitol in [the] presence of a large number of Senators and Representatives. Messrs. Garfield, Cox, of New York, and others, spoke in the phonograph and their voices and speeches were reproduced with remarkable accuracy, the volume and peculiarity of sound and emphasis of each speaker being plainly recognized.

In an interview published in the *Star* Mr. Edison describes a marvelous discovery recently made. He says: "Night before last I found out some additional points about the carbon which I use in my carbon telephone. It may be used as a heat measurer. It will detect one-fifty-thousandth of a degree, Fahrenheit. I don't know but what I can make an arrangement by which the heat of the stars will close the circuit at the proper time automatically and directly. It is a curious idea that the heat of a star millions of miles away should close a circuit on this miserable little earth, but I do not think it impossible."

Of the practical uses for which the phonograph may be made available, Mr. Edison says: "I expect to have my improved phonograph ready in four or five months. This will be useful for many purposes. A business man can speak a letter to the machine, and his office boy, who need not be a shorthand writer, can write it down at any time, as

Edison and His Speaking Machine This portrait was taken by the Mathew Brady Studio during the initial acclaim surrounding the phonograph in 1878. Edison's hand is resting on the crank that turned to operate the primitive recording and playback device.

Courtesy of the Edison National Historic Site, National Park Service, U.S. Department of the Interior.

rapidly or slowly as he desires. Then we mean to use it to enable persons to enjoy good music at home. Say, for instance, that Adelina Patti sings the 'Blue Danube' into the phonograph, we will reproduce the perforated tinfoil on which her singing is impressed, and sell it in sheets. It can be reproduced in any parlor with equal fullness and about one half the original volume. In the same way the tones of a great elocutionist can be preserved. The President of the American Philological Society wants one of my improved phonographs to preserve the accents of the Onondagas and Tuscaroras, who are dying out. One old man speaks the language fluently and correctly, and he is afraid that he will die. The phonograph will preserve the exact pronunciation."

North American Review, **June 1878**

THE PHONOGRAPH AND ITS FUTURE

BY THOMAS A. EDISON

Of all the writer's inventions, none has commanded such profound and earnest attention throughout the civilized world as has the phonograph. This fact he attributes largely to that peculiarity of the invention which brings its possibilities within range of the speculative imaginations of all thinking people, as well as to the almost universal applicability of the foundation principle, namely, the gathering up and retaining of sounds hitherto fugitive, and their reproduction at will.

From the very abundance of conjectural and prophetic opinions which have been disseminated by the press, the public is liable to become confused, and less accurately informed as to the immediate result and effects of the phonograph than if the invention had been one confined to certain specific applications, and therefore of less interest to the masses. The writer has no fault to find with this condition of the discussion of the merits and possibilities of his invention; for, indeed, the possibilities are so illimitable and the probabilities so numerous that he—though subject to the influence of familiar contact—is himself in a somewhat chaotic condition of mind as to where to draw the dividing line. In point of fact, such line cannot with safety be defined in ordinary inventions at so early a stage of their development. In the case of an invention of the nature and scope of the phonograph, it is practically impossible to indicate it today, for tomorrow a trifle may extend it almost indefinitely.

There are, however, certain stages in the developing process which have thus far been actually reached; certain others which are clearly within reach; and others which, though they are in the light of to-day classed as possibilities, may tomorrow become probable, and a little later actual achievements. It is the intention of the writer in this article to confine himself to the actual and the probable, to the end that a clearer conception of the immediate realizations of the phonograph may be had. He concedes to the public press and the world of science the imaginative work of pointing and commenting upon the possible. It is in view of the liberal manner in which this has already been done, and the handsome treatment he has received at their hands, that he for the first time appears in *propria persona* to discuss and comment upon the merits of one of his own inventions. . . .

. . . The several essential features of the phonograph [demonstrate] the following as *faits accomplis:*

1. The captivity of all manner of sound-waves heretofore designated as "fugitive," and their permanent retention.
2. Their reproduction with all of their original characteristics at will, without the presence of consent of the original source, and after the lapse of any period of time.
3. The transmission of such captive sounds through the ordinary channels of commercial intercourse and trade in material form, for purpose of communication or as merchantable goods.
4. Indefinite multiplication and preservation of such sounds, without regard to the existence or non-existence of the original source.
5. The captivation of sounds with or without the knowledge or consent of the source of their origin.

The probable application of these properties of the phonograph and the various branches of commercial and scientific industry presently indicated will require the exercise of more or less mechanical ingenuity. Conceding that the apparatus is practically perfected in so far as the faithful reproduction of sound is concerned, many of the following applications will be made the moment the new form of apparatus, which the writer is now about completing, is finished. These, then, might be classed as actualities; but they so closely trench upon other applications which will immediately follow, that it is impossible to separate them: hence they are all enumerated under the head of probabilities, and each separately considered. . . .

Letter-writing. The apparatus now being perfected in mechanical details will be the standard phonograph, and may be used for all purposes, except such as require a special form of matrix, such as toys, clocks, etc., for an indefinite repetition of the same thing. The main utility of the phonograph, however, being for the purpose of letter-writing and other forms of dictation, the design is made with a view to its utility for that purpose. . . .

The practical application of this form of phonograph for communications is very simple. A sheet of foil is placed in the phonograph, the clock-work set in motion, and the matter dictated into the mouth-piece without other effort than when dictating to a stenographer. It is then removed, placed in a suitable form of envelope, and sent through the ordinary channels to the correspondent for whom designed. He, placing it upon his phonograph, starts his clock-work and *listens* to what his correspondent has to say. Inasmuch as it gives the tone of voice of his correspondent, it is *identified.* As it may be filed away as other letters, and at any subsequent time reproduced, it is a perfect *record.* As two sheets of foil have been indented with the same facility as a single sheet, the "writer" may thus *keep a duplicate* of his communication. As the principal of a business house, or his partners now dictate the important business communications to clerks, to be written out, they are required to do no more by the phonographic method, and do thereby *dispense with the clerk, and maintain perfect privacy* in their communications.

The phonograph letters may be dictated at home, or in the office of a friend, the *presence* of a stenographer *not being required.* The dictation may be as rapid as the thoughts can be formed or the lips utter them. The recipient may listen to his letters being read at a rate of from 150 to 200 words per minute, and at the same time busy himself about other matters. Interjections, explanations, emphasis, exclamations, etc., may be thrown into such letters, *ad libitum.*

In the early days of the phonograph, ere it has become universally adopted, a correspondent in Hong Kong may possibly not be supplied with an apparatus, thus necessitating a written letter of the old-fashioned sort. In that case the writer would use his phonograph simply as a dictating machine, his clerk writing it out from the phonograph at leisure, causing as many words to be uttered at one time as his memory was capable of retaining until he had written them down. The clerk need not be a stenographer, nor need he have been present when the letter was dictated, etc.

The advantages of such an innovation upon the present slow, tedious, and costly methods are too numerous, and too readily suggest themselves, to warrant their enumeration, while there are no disadvantages which will not disappear coincident with the general introduction of the new method.

Dictation. All kinds and manner of dictation which will permit of the application of the mouth of the speaker to the mouthpiece of the phonograph may be as readily effected by the phonograph as in the case of letters. If the matter is for the printer, he would much prefer, in setting it up in type, to use his ears in lieu of his eyes. He has other uses for them. It would even be worthwhile to compel witnesses in court to speak directly into the phonograph, in order to thus obtain an unimpeachable record of their testimony.

The increased delicacy of the phonograph, which is in the near future, will enlarge this field rapidly. It may then include all the sayings of not only the witness, but the judge and the counsel. It will then also comprehend the utterances of public speakers.

Books. Books may be read by the charitably-inclined professional reader, or by such readers especially employed for the purpose, and the record of such a book used in the asylums of the blind, hospitals, the sick-chamber, or even with great profit and amusement by the lady or gentleman whose eyes and hands may be otherwise employed; or, again, because of the greater enjoyment to be had from a book when read by an elocutionist than when read by the average reader. The ordinary record-sheet, repeating this book from fifty to a hundred times as it will, would command a price that would pay the original reader well for the slightly-increased difficulty in reading it aloud in[to] the phonograph.

Educational purposes. As an elocutionary teacher, or as a primary teacher for children, it will certainly be invaluable. By it difficult passages may be correctly rendered for the pupil but once, after which he has only to apply to his phonograph for instructions. The child may thus learn to spell, commit to memory, a lesson set for it, etc., etc.

Music. The phonograph will undoubtedly be liberally devoted to music. A song sung on the phonograph is reproduced with marvelous accuracy and power. Thus a friend may in a morning call sing a song which shall delight an evening company, etc. As a musical teacher it will be used to enable one to master a new air, the child to form its first songs, or to sing him to sleep.

Family record. For the purposes of preserving the sayings, the voices, and *the last words* of the dying member of the family, as of great men, the phonograph will unquestionably outrank the photograph. . . .

Toys. A doll which may speak, sing, cry or laugh, may be safely promised our children for the Christmas holidays ensuing. Every species of animal or mechanical toy, such as locomotives, etc. may be supplied with their natural and characteristic sounds.

Clocks. The phonographic clock will tell you the hour of the day; call you to lunch; send your lover home at ten, etc.

Advertising, etc. This class of phonographic work is so akin to the foregoing that it is only necessary to call attention to it.

Speech and other utterances. It will henceforth be possible to preserve for future generations the voices as well as the words of our Washingtons, our Lincolns, our Gladstones, etc., and to have them give us their "greatest effort" in every town and hamlet in the country, upon our holidays.

Lastly, and in quite another direction, the phonograph will perfect the telephone, and revolutionize present *systems of telegraphy.* That useful invention is now restricted in its field of operation by reason of the fact that it is a means of communication which leaves no record of its transactions, thus restricting its use to simple conversational chitchat, and such unimportant details of business as are not considered of sufficient importance to record. Were this different, and our telephone-conversation automatically recorded, we should find the reverse of the present status of the telephone. It would be expressly resorted to *as* a means of perfect record. In writing our agreements we incorporate in the writing the summing up of our understanding—using entirely new and different phraseology from that which we used to express our understanding of the transaction in its discussion, and not infrequently thus begetting perfectly innocent causes of misunderstanding.

A SUGGESTION.

HOW MUCH BETTER IF, INSTEAD OF HIRSUTE ITALIAN ORGAN-GRINDERS
PARADING OUR STREETS, WE COULD HAVE FAIR FEMALE PHONOGRAPHERS
PLAYING OUR BEST POETS IN THEIR OWN ORIGINAL VOICES !

Punch *Cartoon (1878)* As a machine for recording culture,
Edison's phonograph became immediately entangled in
different meanings of the term. Here a cartoon from the
London magazine *Punch* offers a slur against Italians as
it jokes that England's (highbrow) poets might be
disseminated phonographically, taking the place of
(lowbrow) organ-grinding in the streets of London.
Jersey City Public Library, Jersey City, N.J.

Now, if the telephone, with the phonograph to record its sayings, were used in the preliminary discussion, we would not only have the full record and correct text, but every word of the whole matter capable of throwing light upon the subject. . . .

"How can this application be made?" will probably be asked by those unfamiliar with either the telephone or phonograph.

Both these inventions cause a plate or disk to vibrate, and thus produce sound-waves in harmony with those of the voice of the speaker. A very simple device may be made by which the one vibrating disk may be made to do duty for both the telephone and the phonograph, thus enabling the speaker to *simultaneously transmit and record his message.* What system of telegraphy can approach that? A similar combination at the distant end of the wire enables the correspondent, if he is present to *hear it while it is being recorded.* Thus we have a mere passage of words for the action, but a complete and durable record of those words as the result of that action. Can economy of time or money go further than to annihilate time and space, and bottle up for posterity the mere utterance of man, without other effort on his part than to speak the words? . . .

New York Clipper, **March 16, 1878**

IMPORTANT TO THE PROFESSION

We desire to call attention to the phonograph, a remarkable invention just brought to public notice by Prof. T. A. Edison. By means of this precious little instrument, what you say today may be reproduced in all its purity or impurity *a year or ten years hence!* Just think of it! Through the aid of this machine a manager contracts with a player for an engagement of two, five, or seven weeks; the player corks up the contract in this phonograph. On the opening night of the engagement the player is found to be N.G. — no good; and he is bounced without ceremony. Player sues him for seven weeks' salary; manager denies having engaged him; the poor player uncorks his talking machine, and the very words of the manager are repeated by the phonograph. Of course he gains his case.

Performers have a good deal of spare time through the day — managers can now, by means of this little coffee-mill, cork up songs, and jokes, and sketches rattled off by his people when they are off duty; and should any one of them refuse to go on at night unless the manager will loan him three dollars and a half to buy a duster [a coat], his employer can snap his fingers at him, tell him, in the language of Shakespeare, to "go to," unwind his phonographic cylinder, and the program is carried on without a break—the very tone of voice and mimicry of the actor and singer are given all the same as if the indisposed on stood in the presence of the audience. No more physician's certificates will be necessary—if a prima-donna has an engagement here, and wishes to sing in Havana at the same time, as some of them do, she need only sing her numbers in the mouthpiece of the new contrivance, send it by express to Havana, and the impresario has but to let loose the diaphragmed vocalizations, and out they roll to delight the Habaneros! It's wonderful! With the song-and-dance man there need be no limit to the number of "turns" he can make in one night. In moments of leisure all he has to do is to warble into the mouth of the peanut-roaster "Tommy Make Room for Your Uncle," or any other fashionable ballad, ship it to Philadelphia, or Boston, or Baltimore; and, sure enough, at night while the singer is before us in *propia persona,* he is actually singing the bottled-up song in either or all of the cities named, and salary going on at each place! And what a splendid contrivance it will be for the [recent flop] Count Joannes and his troupe! All they have to do is speak their lines in the mouthpiece of the phonograph, fasten 'em up, and send the machine to the theater at night to grind out the play. Cabbages, eggs, flour, etc. are of no avail; there are no actors in sight [to aim at], and the curtain falls on a discomfited and disconcerted audience. Great triumph for the Count and Avenia!

There is no end to the uses and abuses to which this extraordinary invention can be put. Frinstance [sic], a new play is to be acted at the Fifth-Avenue Theater for the first time on any stage; a man goes there with one of these coffee-mills; as fast as the actors speak their lines the man repeats them at the mouthpiece, and in this way bottles up the whole play, of which Manager Fiske imagines himself to be the possessor of the sole copy! The next night the same play, word for word, is produced at a rival house! Tableau!

Nay, more! A circus clown makes love to the only daughter of the wealthy Mr. Blibbs. She favors his suit; yes, she promises to be his own true bride until death. Clown induces her to repeat her vows of love and affection into the gutta-percha mouth of a clothes-wringer; he clinches them on the diaphragm—incensed father drives him forth— daughter sides with her wealthy parent—clown sues girl for breach of promise—all the parties are in court, and the girl tries to prove an alibi, which is easy enough to do under ordinary circumstances; but comical clown interposes his coffee-mill, turns the crank, and out come the identical words she used in accepting his troth! Father and daughter stand aghast! The jury awards the heart-stricken clown twenty thousand dollars damages! And he seeks some other guileless creature upon whom to play his points for damages.

You see how the new thing works? Why it is destined to create a revolution in society.

Popular Science Monthly, **April 1878**

THE EDISON PHONOGRAPH.

In a certain sense, this "acoustical marvel of the century" is as simple as a grindstone; but, in a scientific point of view, there are subtle questions about it that only trained physicists can appreciate. Prof. Mayer's article upon the subject, in the foregoing pages, besides accurately explaining the mechanism and its operation, points out the delicate complexity of its effects in a way that will interest all curious-minded readers. Mr. Edison, by this invention, has done for sound what Daguerre did for light—made it possible to fix and permanently retain the most fleeting impressions. We pointed out, last month, the marvelous capacities of cold iron, magnetism, and an electric wire; but the capacities of the phonograph are still more marvelous, for, with only a vibrating place, a sheet of tin-foil, and a crank, it is possible to arrest and fix all kinds of sound, and, having preserved them as long as metals will hold their properties, to give them forth again in all their original qualities. The voice, indeed, is somewhat muffled and minified when returned from the iron tongue of the phonograph; but its intonations, inflections, pauses, and quality, are rendered with surprising fidelity. By the simple turning of the crank, the machine talks, sings, shouts, laughs, whistles, and coughs, so naturally and distinctly, that the listener can hardly believe his senses, or escape from the suspicion that there is some ventriloquist hocus-pocus about it, or a little fellow concealed somewhere about the arrangement. But the fact is established, and must be made the most of. A machine, as simple as a coffee-mill, bears a speech or a song, and gives it back as perfectly as it was first uttered by the living organs of voice. And so, again, we have the lesson repeated, with still greater emphasis, that we must raise our estimate of the powers and potencies of "mere dead matter."

New York Daily Graphic, May 9, 1878

EDISONIANA.

A sketch of Edison in *The Graphic* informs us that he dresses very plainly. Nothing odd about that. The wonder is how he can find time to dress at all. —*Cincinnati Breakfast Table.* . . .

The future of the phonograph is thus explained by *Funny Folks:* Ardent lover—"You ask for some proof of my affection, my devotion. What proof can I offer you? Stay! I have it! I am ready to breathe my vows into the Young Ladies' Best Companion, or Breach-of-Promise Self-Registering-Evidence Phonograph! There."

Since Edison invented the telephone and phonograph he has more orders for new inventions than he can attend to. One part wants him to turn his attention to a gas meter that won't always lie in favor of the company; a third desires a pocket-book that will always contain a dollar or two; and while he is about it he might as well infuse some of his inventive genius into a flight of stairs that won't creak like all possessed when a man sneaks into the house at midnight. —*Cincinnati Saturday Night.*

A gentleman from this city went to New Jersey a few days ago and saw Mr. Edison, the inventor of the phonograph. The latter stated that his next invention would probably be a machine by which a perfume could be distinctly smelled 100 miles. If this new machine has not yet been christened, we suggest that smellograph would be a good name for it. The gentleman thought the new invention would afford an immense field for the gratification of revenge, and so it would. If a man gets down on a neighbor, all he has to do is to hang a piece of Limburger across his smellograph and then where is he? Fainted away, probably—if he gets a good, strong sniff. —*Anonymous.*

Weekly (New Jersey) *Fredonian,* June 18, 1878

NEW BRUNSWICK

Edison is so much annoyed by the curiosity-seekers that he has been obliged to give public notice that he can no longer entertain them at his laboratory at Menlo Park, and therefore he will hereafter only receive those who have important business to transact with him. He is in the receipt of from eighty to a hundred letters per day, most of them of no importance to him, and he begs people to hold up and give him a chance to attend to his business. He no longer attempts to even read the bulk of this miscellaneous correspondence, and he cannot pretend to answer one letter out of a dozen which he receives. He is so much annoyed by the miscellaneous crowd of visitors that he has been obliged to "turn night into day," and do the bulk of his work after dark. Of course, if he continues this practice he will soon break down, as his labors are of the most exhausting kind, and interruptions of every sort only tend to annoy and use up his vitality. He therefore begs the people to "let him alone." His laboratory is not intended for a place of exhibition, but for serious thought and hard work. The wishes of such a valuable man certainly should be respected by the public.

A visit to Edison. On Wednesday, the 5th instant, the officers of the New-Jersey Editorial Association held a business meeting in Rahway. Having received an invitation from Thomas A. Edison, the inventor of the Phonograph, after the transaction of their business the Editors drove out to Menlo Park in carriages, and availed themselves of the opportunity of inspecting the celebrated inventor and some of this latest inventions. . . .

3

Electric Light and Power

However it might be represented in the press, invention was Edison's business. The documents in this chapter offer a sense of what that business was. They include newspaper stories, but they also reach behind the news, in telegrams and correspondence, in experimental notes and drawings, in promotional rhetoric and litigious quarrels. Together these documents help to demonstrate how partial and how contrived the public face of invention can be, while also showing the range of private machinations that invention entails.

The newspapers continued to focus on Edison as an individual, although Edison's success with electric light and power distribution was corporate in nature. Not only did Edison succeed in drawing together the men and materials that proved necessary, he succeeded in marshalling financial power and legal expertise. His moneyed backers maneuvered behind the scenes to protect their investments and to control and exploit markets across the United States and abroad. At times they manipulated Edison, just as sometimes he manipulated them. American and British courts got involved repeatedly in arguments over Edison's priority in the field and his corresponding bid for patent rights. Municipalities as well as private individuals watched with interest, unsure of making a commitment to new technology and to new economic structures at the same time.

Edison's Sparks of Interest
Noted in the New York Sun

In September 1878, Edison announced his intention to tackle one of the celebrated technological problems of his day: electric lighting. It is striking that the New York Sun *carried the news under a headline that pro-*

claimed a "big triumph," before Edison had even begun his new project. Electrification was a big idea, one that smacked of utopianism, yet the paper tried to humanize its promise by recounting the doings and sayings of "Professor" Edison.

New York Sun, September 10, 1878

INVENTION'S BIG TRIUMPH

AN ELECTRIC MACHINE THAT WILL TRANSMIT POWER BY WIRE.

THE FORCE OF NIAGARA TO BE TURNED TO USE IN NEW YORK CITY . . .

While visiting the mining regions of the Sierra Nevada and Rocky Mountains in his late Western tour, Prof. Edison was struck with the difficulty there had by miners in drilling and boring, though in many cases in the vicinity of rapid flowing streams. Except in "placer" mines where the ore is washed out of the bed or banks of a river, or where expensive steam drills are used, the work of mining is laborious. While watching miners drilling by hand, a means of facilitating this work evolved itself from Edison's fertile brain. Turning to his intimate friend, Prof. Barker of the University of Pennsylvania, he exclaimed abstractedly, "Why cannot the power of yonder river [pointing to the Platte River on the plains a thousand feet below] be transmitted to these men by electricity?" This thought seemed not to go from Edison's head, and all the way across the plains on their journey home he and his friend "Barky," as he calls him, discussed various problems for the transmission of power.

Before starting for the West, Professor Barker had visited Ansonia, Conn., where his old friend Mr. William Wallace is engaged in the manufacture of electrical machines. . . . He showed Professor Barker an instrument to which he had devoted the best years of his life, but which was yet in crude condition. He is still experimenting with it, but he believed that he would so perfect it as to transmit power from one point to another by means of electricity.

When the Edison party had arrived in New York, Prof. Barker bethought himself of the instrument previously shown him by his friend and which at the time he had only cursorily examined. He invited Prof. Edison to visit Ansonia with him, an invitation that was at once accepted. Last Sunday was the day fixed upon. The party consisted of

Profs. Edison and Barker, Prof. Chandler of the Board of Health, and Mr. Edison's assistant, Mr. Bacheller [sic].

It was an agreeable surprise to the party to find that Mr. Wallace had perfected his machine. Being exceedingly modest and caring not for notoriety, he had shown the instrument to few, and these only persons whose lack of scientific knowledge prevented them from comprehending its usefulness. Mr. Wallace calls it a telemachon, and he smiled with pride as he pointed to a number of these machines, each one an improvement upon its predecessor, and each having required years to design and nearly $1,000 to construct.

Mr. Edison was enraptured. He fairly gloated over it. Then power was applied to the telemachon, and eight electric [arc] lights were kept ablaze at one time, each being equal to 4,000 candles, the subdivision of electric lights being a thing unknown to science. This filled up Mr. Edison's cup of joy. He ran from the instrument to the lights, and from the lights back to the instrument. He sprawled over a table with the simplicity of a child, and made all kinds of calculations. He calculated the power of the instrument and of the lights, the probable loss of power in transmission, the amount of coal the instrument would save in a day, a week, a month, a year, and the result of such savings on manufacturing. . . .

Mr. Edison believes that he can so assist Mr. Wallace in perfecting the telemachon that power may be transmitted from one point to another as though it were a telegraphic message. Already by means of this instrument Mr. Wallace is enabled to transmit the power of the Naugatuck River a quarter of a mile. The power of this stream is great enough to drive the ponderous machinery of the Wallace factory, where 300 men are employed. A series of experiments with the instrument has shown that in the transmission of this enormous power by electricity only 20 percent is lost.

In this instrument the electricity is produced by the Wallace [dynamo], no battery being used. . . .

New York Sun, September 16, 1878

EDISON'S NEWEST MARVEL

SENDING CHEAP LIGHT, HEAT, AND POWER BY ELECTRICITY
ILLUMINATING GAS TO BE SUPERSEDED

EDISON SOLVING THE PROBLEM OF DIVIDING THE TOO GREAT
BRILLIANCY FROM AN ELECTRIC MACHINE.

Mr. Edison says that he has discovered how to make electricity a cheap and practicable substitute for illuminating gas. Many scientific men have worked assiduously in that direction, but with little success. A powerful electric light was the result of these experiments, but the problem of its division into many small lights was a puzzler. Gramme, Siemens, Brush, Wallace, and others produced at most ten lights from a single machine, but a single one of them was found to be impracticable for lighting ought save large foundries, mills, and workshops. It has been reserved for Mr. Edison to solve the difficult problem desired. This, he says, he has done within a few days. His experience with the telephone, however, has taught him to be cautious, and he is exerting himself to protect the new scientific marvel, which, he says, will make the use of gas for illumination a thing of the past.

Mr. Edison, besides his power of origination, has the faculty for developing the ideas and mechanical constructions of others. He visited the Roosevelt pianoforte factory in this city, and, while examining the component parts of the instruments, made four suggestions so valuable that they have been patented. While in the mining district of the West, recently, he devised a means of determining the presence of gold below the surface without resorting to costly and laborious boring and blasting. While on a visit to William Wallace, the electrical machine manufacturer, in Ansonia, Conn., he was shown the lately perfected dynamo-electric machine for transmitting power by electricity. . . .

Edison on returning home after his visit to Ansonia, studied and experimented with electric lights. On Friday last his efforts were crowned with success, and the project that has filled the minds of many scientific men for years was developed.

"I have it now!" he said, on Saturday, while vigorously turning the handle of a Ritchie inductive coil in his laboratory at Menlo Park, "and, singularly enough, I have obtained it through an entirely different process than that from which scientific men have ever sought to secure it. They have all been working in the same groove, and when it is known how I have accomplished my object, everybody will wonder why they have never thought of it, it is so simple. When ten lights have been produced by a single electric machine, it has been thought to be a great triumph of scientific skill. With the process I have just discovered, I can produce a thousand; aye, ten thousand; from one machine. Indeed, the number may be said to be infinite. When the brilliancy and cheapness of the lights are made known to be public; which will be in a few weeks, or just as soon as I can thoroughly protect the process; illumination by carbureted hydrogen gas will be discarded. With fifteen or twenty of these dynamo-electric machines recently perfected by Mr. Wallace I can light the entire lower part of New York City, using a 500 horse power engine. I propose to establish one of these light centers in Nassau Street, whence wires can be run up town as far as the Cooper Institute [near Eighth Street] down to the Battery [at the lower tip of Manhattan], and across to both rivers. These wires must be insulated, and laid in the ground in the same manner as gas pipes. I also propose to utilize the gas burners and chandeliers now in use. In each house I can place a light meter, whence these wires will pass through the house, tapping small metallic contrivances that may be placed over each burner. Then housekeepers may turn off their gas, and send the meters back to the companies whence they came. Whenever it is desired to light a jet, it will only be necessary to touch a little spring near it. No matches are required.

"Again, the same wire that brings the light to you," Mr. Edison continued, "will also bring power and heat. With the power you can run an elevator, a sewing machine or any other mechanical contrivance that requires a motor, and by means of the heat you may cook your food. To utilize the heat, it will only be necessary to have the ovens or stoves properly arranged for its reception. This can be done at trifling cost. The dynamo-electric machine, called a telemachon, . . . may be run by water or steam power at a distance. When used in a large city the machine would of necessity be run by steam power. I have computed the relative cost of the light power and heat generated by the electricity transmitted to the telemachon to be but a fraction of the cost where obtained in the ordinary way. By a battery or steam power it is forty-six times cheaper, and by waterpower probably 95 percent cheaper."

It has been computed that by Edison's process the same amount of light that is given by 1,000 cubic feet of the carbureted hydrogen gas now used in this city, and for which from $2.50 to $3 is paid, may be obtained for from twelve to fifteen cents. Edison will soon give a public exhibition of his new invention.

Money Matters, Original Correspondence

October–December 1878

The announcement that Edison was taking up the matter of electric lighting caused a great stir in some circles and financial markets. Edison himself blustered confidently, while privately his backers and associates all wondered how they might turn the new invention to account. The telegrams and letters excerpted here form a small part of that initial flurry of speculation. Theodore Puskas and George Gouraud were both Europeans involved with promoting Edison's earlier inventions abroad. Both wanted in on electric lighting. Stockton Griffin and Grosvenor Lowrey were American investors who had worked with Edison before and who tried to handle him to their advantage. J. P. Morgan (who wrote to his uncle, Walter Burns) was an important American financier.

Edison to Theodore Puskas, October 5, 1878

MENLO PARK, N.J.

My Dear Puskas:
. . . The Electric light is going to be a great success.

I have something *entirely new;* Wm H Vanderbilt and friends have taken it in this country and on Monday next advance $50,000 to conduct experiments.

I retain ½ half of the capital stock of the Co they are to form and also receive a royalty of $30,000 yearly if it proves more economical than gas which *I am certain it will do.* Vanderbilt is the largest gas stock owner in America.

Carbon telephones great success here. I furnish 200 carbon buttons daily to manufacturers (several firms being engaged) making them for the Western Union.

I propose to send you through Gouraud a sample of each kind. I do not send them direct for fear of the French patent law, on the subject of imported articles patented in France;

Very Truly,
Thomas A. Edison.

Telegram from George Gouraud in London, to Edison, October 7, 1878

Edison

Panic in gas shares. Electric light occupying much public discussion large combinations forming to work it but hesitate which system to adopt. How soon can Adams show your system here. If you will cable what it is desirable to say about it, if anything I will publish such a letter in leading newspapers as will at least delay anybody's purchasing until your system can be seen.

Gouraud

Edison Reply to Gouraud, October 8, 1878

Gouraud. Say nothing publicly about light. Let them go ahead. I have only correct principle. Requires six months to work up the details. Gas men here hedged by going in with me. . . .

J. P. Morgan to Walter Burns, October 30, 1878

NEW YORK

My Dear Walter,
I have been very much engaged for several days past on a matter which is likely to prove most important to us all not only as regards its importance to the world at large but to us in particular in a pecuniary point of view. Secrecy at the moment is so essential that I do not dare put it on paper. Subject is Edison's Electric light — importance can be realized from the editorials in London Times & other papers & the effect upon gas stocks which have declined from 25-50% since rumors of Edison's success. It is not unlikely that I may cable for you to come

to London . . . this matter needs careful handling if anything comes of it. It is not entirely certain—I shall do nothing until it is—but when that time comes . . . we must be prepared to strike. I fear father will think I am imagining but I am sure he will change his mind.

J. Pierpont Morgan

Stockton Griffin to Grosvenor Lowrey, November 1, 1878

CONFIDENTIAL

Dear Sir,

Upon arriving at the Park yesterday I spoke to Mr. Edison regarding our conversation about the Sawyer-man Electric light, being careful not to say anything beyond what you told me; I was astonished at the manner in which Mr. E received the information. He was visibly agitated and said it was the old story; i.e., lack of confidence; the same experience which he had had with the telephone, and in fact with all of his *successful* inventions, was being re-enacted. He also referred to the telephone being loaded down with useless encumbrances and remarked that if he had a voice in the matter the electric light should not be so treated; no combinations, no consolidations for him; I do not feel at liberty to repeat all that he said, but I do feel impelled to respectfully suggest that as little be said to him as possible in regard to the matter. He said it was to be expected that everyone who had been working in this direction, or had any knowledge of the subject, would immediately set up their claims upon ascertaining that his system was likely to be perfect. All this he anticipated but had no fears of the result knowing that the line he was developing was entirely original and out of the rut.

I was careful to say to him that as far as you were concerned there was no lack of confidence but that perhaps this element could be found in Mr. Edison and others. He will no doubt give you his views in full so I will abstain from saying more at present but will try and find time to call on you the next time I visit the City and say more on the subject as I consider it somewhat serious.

Very Truly,
S. L. Griffin

Grosvenor Lowrey to Edison, December 10, 1878

NEW YORK

My Dear Edison:

The visit yesterday [by financial backers to Menlo Park] was productive, I think, of solid good results. Our friends had their imaginations somewhat tempered; but their judgments are instructed, and we now have to deal with an intelligent comprehension of things as they are, which makes both your part and mine much easier. They realize now that you are doing a man's work upon a great problem and they think you have got the jug by the handle with a reasonable probability of carrying it safely to the well and bringing it back full.

In respect to Mr. Puskas my situation and that of Drexel, Morgan & Co is a delicate one. They desire very much to control the light in all parts of Europe believing that by making one job of it, with headquarters here, the general result will be more satisfactory in every way. I suggest to you some reasons for thinking it so much more for your interest to deal with them than with people residing on the other side, as to make it proper for you to write in full to Mr. Puskas enforcing your former proposition to him.

First. Before this light is introduced anywhere it must be exhibited in various places in Europe, say, for instance, London, Paris, Vienna and, perhaps, Berlin. These exhibitions should be under one control, and, to be made successful, must have your direction while preparing to make them; and considering all the numerous questions which will from time to time arise, you will be much better off if you are dealing with your own people here, at home, with the opportunity for constant consultation comparison of views &c &c.

Second: When we come to the business of disposing of the patents it may be good financial policy not to sell outright, but to reserve interests in different places, to balance one thing against another, and to draw the largest result by allowing time &c. To do this rightly requires an amount of skill and power which neither you nor I possess, but which may be possessed by a great many bankers and financial people living here and in Europe.

But, for your purposes, it ought to be a matter of the greatest comfort to have your partners, who are to account to you, *right here,* at your own home; people whom you can know all about, and whom you can reach by legal process if they treat you wrongly. By this means, also, you keep, through them, a controlling hand upon the development of the invention on the other side so as to enforce your views & wishes, and there may arise many occasions upon which you will be very thankful that everything is managed and controlled at the corner of Wall and Broad Streets, within twenty miles of your own office. Besides that, Americans and Englishmen, as Mr. Fabbri said the other day, are a different kind of men to deal with from Continental people. I believe from my own experience that Americans are the honestest and most straightforward, as well as the best-hearted people in the world. I think the English are next. An American Banker, residing in Paris, once told me he longed to get back to the United States for it seemed to him as if you could deal openly and above-board with people in New York while in Paris, where he resided, there was no chicanery or trick considered to be beneath a great banker; & that it was only by having the skill to watch them, and guard yourself at all points, that it was possible to do business with them.

Of course if you had a completed thing which you were willing to sell at a given price there would be no difficulty; but if you require a given price down it must be a small one; or, if you reserve interests in the future development, in order to get the larger price, you will be entirely at the mercy of people who are not only personally but by habit, education, and general ideas, strangers to you.

Drexel, Morgan & Co have their own means and agencies for matching such people, and also the power, like any other strong banking house, to force the respect of these people. They expect to see them and do business with them again.

Third: It is altogether probable that you will require more money. How much more neither you nor anybody else can tell. If you were to get some sum now, even as much as $50,000, from Mr. Puskas (and if you get any amount it should be expressly stipulated that it is subject to all the risks of the business), you cannot know that that will be enough. You may bring this up to a point where Anthony J. Drexel, and men like him, will clearly see that the thing is *sure,* but that it requires, in order to put it to a test in Cities, the outlay of hundreds of thousands of dollars. If that time should come the money will be forthcoming, (if only required to find out the best method of doing an assured thing). In that case you would want all your assets here. If you should in the meantime have parted with your right to the Continental Countries it might very much cripple you.

To sum the whole matter up, you are now in the best conceivable position which the circumstances permit. You are introduced to a new class of men who entertain the highest confidence in your ability and respect for your character. They possess all the means which may ever be required; they live here, speak your own language, share your ideas as to what is honest and upright; are conveniently at hand to act as partners with you upon every question touching the preliminary development and subsequent management of what we all think is to be a great property. They supply precisely everything which you are lacking, and possess all the European influence, or the means of getting at such influence, which can ever be required.

Upon these considerations, if you are so disposed, I think you might fairly write to Mr. Puskas and say that *he owes to your position some consideration;* that while 10% is not as much as 50%, and while it may be true that his friends possess more European influence than yours, yet yours possess *sufficient,* and, upon all *other considerations,* are preferable, for your purposes, to his; and ten per cent of what they will get is a very large return for what he has done, and one for which he ought to be very grateful, while the outcome which *you* may expect from dealing through your friends instead of his is vastly beyond the proportion of ten to fifty. I think you might with propriety say all these things to him and urge that he who obtains so considerable an interest, as is now proposed, for so small an outlay, and for merely receiving a telegraphic dispatch, ought gracefully to yield when he finds your position, generally, requires the change.

I repeat that I feel a delicacy in pressing you about this because, of course, you know that I expect Drexel Morgan & Co to give me some portion of their profits, and I do not wish to crowd Mr. Puskas any more than I should wish anybody to crowd me nor will I do so by seeking to exercise any influence upon your determination due to the fact that I am nearer to you than he is. I therefore lay these suggestions before you as rational considerations fairly affecting your own interest. I confess I should feel, however, if Drexel Morgan & Co were not to get the Continental business, that you had thrown away one of your strong cards. I do not mean to say that their interest would relax, for they would still have the American interest and the English business which would be very great, and probably plenty to satisfy them so far as the profits go; but I think they are very proud of the idea of swinging the whole thing for Europe; it seems to enlist them as the champions and representatives, and you know how men act under such motives.

Truly Yours,
G. P. L.

Experimental Notes

January 1879

By the beginning of 1879, Edison and his team were searching vigorously for the right material for filaments. Notes like this one (handwritten by Edison) show them trying many different metals, keeping careful track of how each behaved as a "burner." Here they react excitedly to the properties of nickel (Ni), although their hopes were eventually dashed. This note is one of the first notebook entries to hint at the impending trials of incandescence in a vacuum: Edison here mentions that the nickel can be prevented from burning away if "sealed," presumably in a glass bulb. These entries further demonstrate some of the physical discomforts of inventing. Edison and his employees regularly put in long hours, but now they hurt their eyes looking into brilliant electric arcs and torches.

MENLO PARK, N.J.
JANUARY 22, 1879

We now commence some experiments [using a blow torch]. . . .

Iron instantly melts and oxidizes, but I think the extra heat due to its oxidation is the cause of its melting. Cobalt is very difficult to melt; it oxidizes slightly. Nickel is exceedingly difficult to melt and I think it has as high a melting point as platinum and possibly higher if fused in a vacuum and prevented from oxidizing. A globule of nickel in molten state was brilliantly incandescent and did not appear to oxidize or grow smaller. Silicum does not fuse but at a certain temperature it oxidizes with explosion. Boron does not fuse or apparently oxidize. . . .

We take a piece of nickel and roll it out cut a narrow strip and pass a current through it and very strange to say it becomes brilliantly incandescent without fusing. I think it nearly if not equal to platinum. It slowly oxidizes but we shall prevent this by sealing the burner [in a vacuum]. When it does fuse it acts like the Platinum-Iridium 20% alloy. It remains hard when incandescent. It is very probable that absolute chemically pure nickel will have a very much higher fusing point than the sample we have, which is probably only commercial. This is a great discovery for electric Light, in the way of economy [since nickel is so much cheaper than platinum] . . .

JANUARY 27TH.

Last 3 days been arranging our apparatus for conducting experiments. With Ott, Batchelor is now experimenting.

I have rigged up two carbon points with the Gramme [generator] and concentrate the [electrical] arc in a lime crucible [where the metal to be tested is put].

Melted nickel and preserved it in a bottle for future experiments. Also alloy Ca & Ni. Also Ni & Fe. Also large quantity of Fe with small quantity Ni.

Owing to enormous power of the light my eyes commenced to pain after 7 hours work and I had to quit.

JANUARY 28, 1879

Suffered the pains of hell with my eyes last night from 10 P.M. till 4 A.M. when got to sleep with a big dose of Morphine, eyes getting better & do not pain much at 4 P.M. but I lose today.

Francis Upton, Letters Home

November 1878–April 1879

Edison's financial backers pressed him to research what had been done on electricity before, rather than to push ahead brashly on his own. They wanted assurances that he was coming up with something new (and therefore patentable and valuable). To do the research, Edison hired a young physics student named Francis R. Upton, who had studied at Princeton and abroad, with one of the great scientists of Europe, Hermann von Helmholtz. Though far superior to Edison in his knowledge of science and mathematics, Upton was awed by the inventor. He quickly became comfortable in Menlo Park and part of Edison's trusted team of immediate associates. His frequent letters home to his parents are some of the most intimate accounts that exist of the laboratory in these months of frenzied experimentation. A small number are excerpted in three chronological groups in this chapter.

NOVEMBER 7, 1878

Dear Mother:

I have asked if I could have a place [at Menlo Park] and am to receive an answer Saturday. At first I will have a desk in the office and do

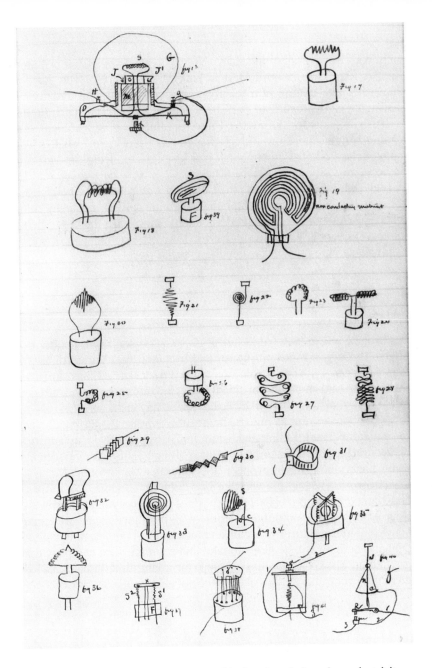

Twenty-Six Ideas for Burners (1878) In his first frenzied work on electricity, Edison drew these possible "burners" for use inside his lamp. He wanted to try everything.

Courtesy of the Edison National Historic Site, National Park Service, U.S. Department of the Interior.

such work as may fall to my share. No pay to start with. That is if anything is found for me to do I shall have it. Afterwards I may have a chance to take charge of a telephone system in some city. At first I shall have clerical work to do. The struggle has been a hard one to give up my plans for the future. I have dreamt of being a student and leading a quiet life, now I shall change all. I feel sure I shall make many failures but I hope none bad enough to bring me in bad name. . . .

I felt that though [studying in] Germany would be extremely pleasant, yet it would be much more like getting settled in life to commence doing something. There I would only learn how to spend money; here I will learn how to earn it. . . . Everyone must work and it is not always the most agreeable thing in the world. . . .

FEB 23, 1879

Dear Father:

Yesterday I was in New York. I went in Friday to see about getting my effects through the custom house and to attend the Alumni dinner. I found the ways of the custom house very dark. I tried hard to tread them alone and unaided but finally gave up the attempt and hired a broker. I shall have to go in again some day next week so as to arrange about paying as my goods must be appraised and I shall have to sign some paper. I think no custom house in the world can compare with ours for the science of not doing things. This evening when I came back, about 8:30 I went to the laboratory and found Mr. E— hard at work. He told me what he had been doing since I went away and wanted me to criticize. The light does not yet shine as bright as I wish it might but I am not despairing at all but that success will come sometime in the future. Whether it comes or not I am learning a great deal and nothing will be likely to take that from me. The company that are behind Mr. E—mean to stay there for a long time to come and to give him every chance to make a success. . . .

MARCH 2, 1879

Dear Father:

. . . I feel that I am able to take care of myself, trusting to the future. I find my work very pleasant here and not much different from the times when I was a student. The strangest thing to me is the $12 that I

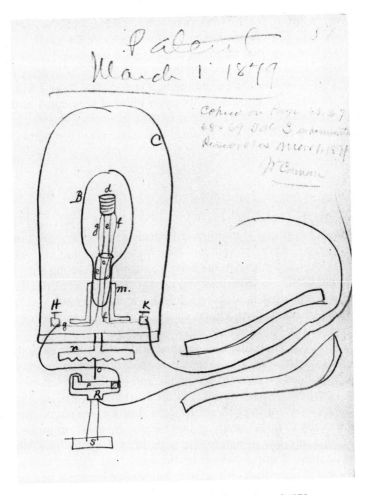

Lamp with Pneumatic Regulator During the spring of 1879, as Edison worked on dynamos and other system components, he continued to experiment with electric lamps like this one, which possessed a complicated regulating device to keep its "burner" from burning. A much simpler lamp was possible after Edison obtained the means of satisfactorily evacuating glass bulbs to make a vacuum.

Courtesy of the Edison National Historic Site, National Park Service, U.S. Department of the Interior.

get each Saturday, for my labor does not seem like work but like study and I enjoy it. The electric light I think will come in time and then be a success; how long that time will be is quite a question. I think that it will be successful eventually, and then my place will be secure. I learn much every week and soon, that is in a year or two think I will be an expert in electrical questions. My pay I know is very small in dollars but the chance to get knowledge is beyond measure. I hope I can earn some money indirectly by writing, and also make my name better known. . . .

———

APRIL 27, 1879

Dear Father:

This month is nearly through and I hardly know where the time has gone, though I have learned and done quite an amount. Mr. [Edison] was sick during the past week for three days and during that time I had a fine chance to experiment to my satisfaction. One thing is quite noticeable here that the work is only a few days behind Mr. Edison, for when he was sick the shop was shut evenings as the work was wanting to keep the men busy. . . .

There still is hope that this summer will see a public exhibition of the electric light. There are thousands of difficulties to be overcome yet before it can be given to the public and Mr. Edison will overcome them if any[one] does. I have not in the least lost my faith in him for I see how wonderful the powers he has, sure for invention. He holds himself ready to make anything that he may be asked to make if it is not against any law of nature. He says he will either have what he wants or prove it impossible. If he does not have a lamp to use electricity he will show that with present knowledge it cannot be had. . . .

Experimental Notes

October 1879

By October 1879 Edison was getting close to a practical bulb. Having studied and rejected platinum, nickel, and other metals, he and his associates were struggling with carbon as a material for filaments. Carbon or carbonized materials were already burnt, and they were kept from burning away completely by being placed in evacuated glass bulbs. It seemed like the right arrangement, but there were still so many other variables to work out. What shape? What material? How carbonized?

How arranged? How protected? Charles Batchelor handwrote these notes in one of Edison's many notebooks. An Englishman, Batchelor served as Edison's right-hand man in much of his electrical experimentation.

Spiral of Carbon, October 7, 1879

MOULD FOR CARBON SPIRAL

Spiral must be .18 long. Inside diameter .1875 or ³⁄₁₆. Outside diameter .207 [inch].

Made a mould for squeezing. Put in some of Wallace's soft carbon and squeezed it out of a hole .02 diameter getting it out a yard long if required. Could make more even, sticks, by rolling on a glass plate with piece of very smooth wood. These sticks could be rolled down to .01 and then wound in spirals. We made some and baked them at a red heat for 15 minutes in a closed tube. When taken out they were hard and solid, much more so than we expected and not at all altered in shape.—A spiral made of *burnt lampblack* [like the sticky black deposit left by a gas lamp]! Mixed with a little tar was even better than the Wallace mixture. . . .

Electric Light, October 22, 1879, 9 A.M.

CARBON SPIRALS

We made some very interesting experiments on straight carbons made from cotton thread so. . . . We took a piece of 6 cord thread no. 24s which is about 13 thousandths in thickness and after fastening to Platinum wires we carbonized it in a closed chamber. We put it in a bulb and in vacuo. It gave a light equal to about ½ candle 18 cells carbon. It had resistance of 133 ohms at starting & afterward went up to 140, probably due to vibration.

Electric Light, October 22, 1879

CARBON LAMPS

Carbonizing process. We made lamps in same manner

1 of Vulcanized fiber
2—Thread rubbed with tarred lampblack
3—Soft paper

4—Fish line
5—Fine thread plaited together 6 strands
6—Soft paper saturated with tar
7—Tar & lampblack with half its bulk of finely divided line work down to .020—straight one ½ inch
8—200's 6 cord 8 strand
9—. . . 6 cord no coating of any kind
10—Cardboard
11—Cotton soaked in tar (boiling) & put in.

No. 2 lamp [the one made with "thread rubbed with tarred lampblack" listed above] had on 18 cells and gave an elegant light equal to about 22 candles.

No. 9 ordinary thread coats 6 cord 24s. Came up to ½ candle and was put on 18 cells battery permanently at 1:30 A.M. . . .

No. 10 Considerable resistance. Equals 1 gas jet. Had small arc in—

No. 9 On from 1:30 A.M. till 3 P.M.: 13½ hour and was then raised to [level of] 3 gas jets for 1 hour, then cracked glass & busted.

ELECTRIC LIGHT

Carbonization. I carbonized the following substances in closed tube at red heat:

1. Vulcanized fiber
2. Celluloid
3. Boxwood shavings
4. Cocoa nut hair and shell
5. Drawing paper No. 1
6. Architects' drawing paper
7. Drawing paper sample 30-3
8. Drawing paper sample 3
9. Spruce shavings
10. Hickory shavings
11. Baywood shavings
12. Cedar (red) shavings
13. Rosewood
14. Fish line . . .

Lamps, October 28, 1879

12. Eight thicknesses of 200s thread twisted and lampblacked a little, length of incandescent surface 3.5 inch——Shit!!! Busted by [Ludwig] Boehm
    Made new carbonizing chamber.
13. 8 thicknesses of 200s thread twisted & blackened a little, length of surface 3.40 inch. Busted by [Ludwig] Boehm . . .

Francis Upton, Letters Home

October–November 1879

As the research continued at Menlo Park, Francis Upton's letters home continued to shed light on the processes of invention and the vagaries of financial backing.

OCTOBER 26, 1879

Dear Father:
This week has brought nothing very new. The electric light is looking up for we have had some very good lamps. The latest gossip that Mr. Edison has told me, is that there is talk of swallowing the old Electric Light Co. in a new one and making the capital three millions of dollars. This new company will be floated by Drexal [*sic*] Morgan & Co. of New York. There is no hope of such a thing until Mr. Edison has given an exhibition. So he is going to try and show some lamps here in the course of a few weeks. I think I shall have some of them in my new house. Our parlor looks splendidly. The piano you gave us helps immensely to furnish it and fills up the corner of the room very well. . . .

———

NOVEMBER 2, 1879

Dear Father:
The Electric light is coming up. We have had a fine burner made of a piece of carbonized thread which gave a light of two or three gas jets. Mr. Edison now proposes to give an exhibition of some lamps in actual operation. There is talk if he can show a number of lamps of

organizing a large company with three or five millions capital to push the matter through. I have been offered $1000 for five shares of my stock . . . Edison says the stock is worth a thousand dollars a share or more, yet he is always sanguine and his valuations are on his hopes more than on his realities.

I am going to New York tomorrow early to buy a few books and to go with Lizzie [Upton's wife] to see if we can get a girl [to hire as a servant]. . . .

NOVEMBER 16, 1879

Dear Father:

. . . Just at the present I am very much elated at the prospects of the Electric Light. During the past week Mr. Edison has succeeded in obtaining the first lamp that answers the purpose we have wished for. It is cheap, much more so than we even hoped to have. The light is obtained from a piece of charred fiber which is bent thus

The burner is made from common card board and cut to about the size shown. This is then sealed in a glass bulb and the air exhausted and then a current of electricity passed through it which heats it to brilliant whiteness so that it will give a light equal to that from a good sized gas burner.

The making of such a burner has made the stock of the Electric Light Co. advance in value. $400 has been offered for shares and there are no sellers. The last week has made all my prospects very bright and I hope they will continue so. I expect that there will be an exhibition given in the course of a few weeks. The wires are laid to my home and I shall light up my parlor. . . .

As matters are turning out I am glad over and over again that I did not spend the year in Germany for I now am put in the way of getting a living far beyond what I there dreamed was possible. I am a thorough master of all that is concerned so far in making a good light. . . .

Experimental Notes

December 1879–January 1880

Edison, Charles Batchelor, and the experimenters at Menlo Park continued to struggle with bulbs and filaments throughout December and well into the new year, even though the press announced "Edison's triumph" in December, 1879, and a grand public exhibition of the "finished" light took place on New Year's Eve. These notes were written by Batchelor in one of Edison's experimental notebooks. Sensitive to the importance of their work, Batchelor was careful to date and sign his entries, many of which refer to individually numbered light bulbs being tested for performance and endurance. Notes from January 2, 1880, do not differ in form or in tone from those written in mid-December 1879, before the hoopla.

General Faults, December 4, 1879

We notice that some of the bulbs are perfectly clear after burning up and using, while others are covered with black. This may be from the fact that some may be better carbonized than others and those not carbonized are brought to higher heat in vacuo & give out more stuff that coats the glass. —Chas. Batchelor . . .

Test of E Light, December 5, 1879

On Dec 3 we made a test at Edison's house at which Mr. Fabbri and party saw it. We lit 2 three light chandeliers, 1 two light ditto, and ran the sewing machine and hand lamp. All went off perfectly with the exception that I put in one lamp and the wires projected too far and made an arc on brass underneath. This did not hurt the lamp. —Chas. Batchelor . . .

Lamps, December 15, 1879

Lamps nos. 200 and 202 had been burning about 4 hours on Dec. 16 and 1 hour on Dec. 17 when both busted as in sketch. . . . Upton suggests that it may be in the focus of the curve of the glass. It does not seem to be exactly in the focus of the curve of the other side of [the filament] loop. They were burning at about 5 or 6 gas jets. —Chas. Batchelor

Faults, December

250. Glass busted, wires melted out.
201. Busted in carbon ¼ above regular place . . .
259. Carbon busted in regular place.
252. Carbon busted in regular place.

January 2, 1880

No. 167. I saw bust, and inside glass broke and in platina clamp falling together crossed and burnt out the [illegible] of chandelier. Burnt 8 hours.
217. Burnt 4 days. Chandelier over Griff.'s desk. Broke ¼ inch above regular place, probably bad vacuum. Edison brought this to me.

Francis Upton, Letters Home

December 1879–January 1880

Francis Upton's letters of December 1879 and January 1880 offer another glimpse of the excitement and the financial speculation that attended Edison's work as he began to demonstrate its elements publicly.

DEC. 21, 1879

Dear Father:
Today has been quite exciting here since this morning's *Herald* contained an account of the discovery of the lamp and the whole invention. Mr. Edison had allowed a *Herald* reporter to take full notes so as to prepare his account for the exhibition which was to come off in a few weeks. The reporter was Edison's friend and he thought he could keep a secret. Yet newspaper traditions were too strong and he sold out at a good price I suppose, for he had the first full account. Mr. Edison is very much provoked and is working off his surplus energy today. The light is very fine and promises much money, yet all is promise. I have my parlor lighted very beautifully with it. Lizzie has

fixed the lamps with ribbons and flowers and I think I am a peg ahead of any one in the show, for all the other lamps are to be put in gas fixtures and follow old customs. Edison thinks people will like the gas fixtures best as they can thus better compare the light given. . . .

Dec 28, 1879

Dear Father:

The electric light is way up. Stock was sold yesterday for $3,500 a share. It is an enormous price for a share the par value of which is only $100. . . .

Mr. Edison has simply found one of the finest things of the age, how to get a good pure light cheaply. . . .

Last night we had an exhibition and several million dollars of capital were represented. Every[thing] went off splendidly. We had over forty gas jet burners running from one machine.

I had a number of gentlemen in my parlor among them the correspondent of the London *Times*. He made a note of my chandelier, which Lizzie will tell you of, so that I may soon read of her decorations in the foreign papers. . . .

January 25, 1880

Dear Father:

The electric light is growing better constantly. I have now a light over my desk so that I am writing you this letter by the light from a little horseshoe [filament]. There is now a burner in my bedroom so that now I do not have to fumble after matches but simply to touch a plug so as to procure a light to wash and dress by. Mr. Edison is going on with his plans for making a large factory here to make electric lamps. . . . The lamps are now lasting as long as can be expected for some have been burning since they were first made and are yet good. One lamp has burned 550 hours and a number are now approaching 500 hours and all those lamps are without the improvements that have been made during the past few weeks which will tend to make them far more durable. . . .

Your loving son,
Francis R. Upton

New York Herald

December 21, 1879

As Francis Upton noted in his letter of the same day, the New York Herald *scooped the rest of the press corps in announcing Edison's new incandescent bulb, which the inventor planned to demonstrate at Menlo Park
on New Year's Eve. Upton reports that Edison was upset by this premature announcement. Why might he have been upset? The paper
recounted the whole long story of Edison's experimentation in heroic
terms and boasted "complete details" of an invention that it implied was
finished and perfected.*

EDISON'S LIGHT. The Great Inventor's Triumph in Electric Illumination.
A SCRAP OF PAPER. It Makes a Light, Without Gas or Flame, Cheaper
Than Oil. Transformed in the Furnace. Complete Details of the Per-
fected Carbon Lamp. FIFTEEN MONTHS OF TOIL. Story of His Tireless
Experiments with Lamps, Burners, and Generators. SUCCESS IN A COT-
TON THREAD . . .

The near approach of the first public exhibition of Edison's long
looked for electric light, announced to take place on New Year's Eve at
Menlo Park, on which occasion that place will be illuminated with the
new light, has revived public interest in the great inventor's work, and
throughout the civilized world scientists and people generally are anx-
iously awaiting the result. From the beginning of his experiments in
electric lighting to the present time Mr. Edison has kept his laboratory guardedly closed, and no authoritative account (except that published in the HERALD some months ago relating to his first patent) of
any of the important steps of his progress has been made public—a
course of procedure the inventor found absolutely necessary for his
own protection. The HERALD is now, however, enabled to present to
its readers a full and accurate account of his work from its inception to
its completion.

A LIGHTED PAPER

Edison's electric light, incredible as it may appear, is produced from a
little piece of paper—a tiny strip of paper that a breath would blow

Drawing of a Successful Lamp (December 1879) This lamp used a carbonized paper filament. Despite this "triumph," trumpeted in the press, laboratory notebooks indicate that Edison, Batchelor, and others at Menlo Park continued to struggle with different lamps into the new year.

Courtesy of the Edison National Historic Site, National Park Service, U.S. Department of the Interior.

away. Through this little strip of paper is passed an electric current, and the result is a bright, beautiful light, like the mellow sunset of an Italian autumn.

"But paper instantly burns, even under the trifling heat of a tallow candle!" exclaims the skeptic, "and how, then, can it withstand the fierce heat of an electric current?" Very true, but Edison makes the little piece of paper more infusible than platinum, more durable than granite. And this involves no complicated process. The paper is merely baked in an oven until all its elements have passed away except its carbon framework. The latter is then placed in a glass globe connected with the wires leading to the electricity producing machine, and the air exhausted from the globe. Then the apparatus is ready to give out a light that produces no deleterious gases, no smoke, no offensive odors—a light without flame, without danger, requiring no matches to ignite, giving out but little heat, vitiating no air, and free from all flickering: a light that is a little globe of sunshine, a veritable Aladdin's lamp. And this light, the inventor claims, can be produced cheaper than that from the cheapest oil. Were it not for the phonograph, the quadruplex telegraph, the telephone and the various other remarkable productions of the great inventor the world might well hesitate to accept his assurance that such a beneficent result had been obtained, but, as it is, his past achievements in science are sufficient guarantee that his claims are not without foundation, even though for months past the press of Europe and America has teemed with dissertations and expositions from learned scientists ridiculing Edison and showing that it was impossible for him to achieve that which he has undertaken.

HIS FIRST ATTENTION TO ELECTRIC LIGHTING

When Edison began his experiments in September 1878, he had just returned from the inspiring scenery of the Rocky Mountains, where he had been enjoying a little recreation after several months of hard labor. He was ripe for fields and enterprises new. A visit to a Connecticut factory where an electric light was used concentrated his thoughts on the subject of lighting by electricity, and he determined to attack the problem. Previous to this time, although he had roamed broadcast over the domain of electricity, wresting from it, as is well known, many of its hidden secrets, Edison had scarcely thought of the subtle fluid in connection with practical illumination. Now, however, he bent all his energies on the subject, and was soon deep in the bewildering intricacies of subdivision, magnetic currents, resistance laws and the various other branches going to make up a system of lighting by electricity. The task before the young inventor was divisible into two parts.

> *First*—The producing of a pure, steady and reliable light from electricity; and
> *Second*—Producing it so cheaply that it could compete with gas for general illumination.

HE CHOOSES INCANDESCENCE

Of the two systems before him—viz. voltaic arc and incandescence systems, Edison chose the latter as his field of operations. Prominent among the difficulties incident to incandescent lighting, it will be remembered, was the liability of the platinum (when that metal was used) to melt under the intense heat of the electric current, and the liability of the carbon, when that was employed, to gradually become dissipated under the combined action of gases and the electric current.

THE PLATINUM LIGHT

As between platinum and carbon as the substance to be made incandescent, Edison took up platinum and devoted first his attention to the obtaining of some device to prevent the platinum from melting under the intense heat of the electric current. An ingenious and simple contrivance met the requirement. He arranged a small lever, about three inches long, so that the expansion of the platinum (caused by the heat) beyond a certain degree would close [the lever], such closing making a new passage for the electric current and cutting it off from the incandescent platinum. When the latter contracted, as it did the moment the heat was lessened, the lever returned to its normal position and allowed the electric current to again pass through the platinum. By this [self-regulating] device the inventor hoped to be able to keep the incandescent platinum always below its melting point. . . .

Numerous other devices of a similar character were tried and for a while they all worked satisfactorily, but the inventor finally discovered that the constant expansion of the [platinum] and its pressure upon the [regulating lever] bent it so that it became unreliable and it was, therefore, abandoned. . . .

THE CRACKS IN PLATINUM

After scores of new experiments he arrived at the true causes of the defects and hastened to apply the remedy. "I have found," he writes, "that when wires or sheets of platinum, iridium or other metallic conductors of electricity that fuse at a high temperature are exposed to a high temperature near their melting point in air for several hours by passing a current of electricity through them and then are allowed to cool, the metal is found to be ruptured, and under the microscope there are revealed myriads of cracks in various directions, many of which reach nearly to the center of the wire. I have also discovered that, contrary to the received notion, platinum or platinum and iridium alloy loses weight when exposed to the heat of a candle; that even heated air causes it to lose weight; that the loss is so great a hydrogen flame is tinged green [by the oxidizing platinum]. After a time the metal falls to pieces; hence wire or sheets of platinum or platinum and iridium alloy as now known in commerce are useless for giving light by incandescence [unless oxidation is prevented by placing them in a vacuum]. . . ."

THE FIRST PLATINUM VACUUM LAMP

About this time another truth dawned upon the inventor—namely, that economy in the production of light from incandescence demanded that the incandescent substance should offer a very great resistance to the passage of the electric current. Concerning this the inventor writes: "It is essential to reverse the present practice of having lamps of but one or two ohms (electrical units) resistance and construct lamps which, when giving their proper light, shall have at least two hundred ohms resistance. . . ."

PERFECTING THE MACHINERY

The lamp, after these latter improvements, was in quite a satisfactory condition, and the inventor contemplated with much gratification the near conclusion of his labors. One by one he had overcome the many difficulties that lay in his path. He had brought up platinum as a substance for illumination from a state of comparative worthlessness to one well nigh perfection. He had succeeded, by a curious combination and improvement in air pumps, in obtaining a vacuum of nearly one millionth of an atmosphere, and he had perfected a generator or electricity producing machine (for all the time he had been working at lamps he was also experimenting in magneto-electric machines) that gave out some ninety per cent in electricity of the energy it received from the driving engine. In a word, all the serious obstacles toward the success of incandescent electric lighting, he believed, had melted away, and there remained but a comparatively few minor details to be arranged before his laboratory was to be thrown open for public inspection and the light given to the world for better or for worse.

A GREAT DISCOVERY

There occurred, however, at this juncture a discovery that materially changed the system and gave a rapid stride toward the perfect electric lamp. Sitting one night in his laboratory reflecting on some of the unfinished details, Edison began abstractedly rolling between his fingers a piece of compressed lampblack mixed with tar for use in his telephone. For several minutes his thoughts continued far away, his fingers in the meantime mechanically rolling out the little piece of tarred lampblack until it had become a slender filament. Happening to glance at it the idea occurred to him that it might give good results as a burner if made incandescent. A few minutes later the experiment was tried, and, to the inventor's gratification, satisfactory, although not surprising results were obtained. Further experiments were made, with altered forms and composition of the substance, each experiment demonstrating that at last the inventor was upon the right track.

A COTTON THREAD

A spool of cotton thread lay on the table in the laboratory. The inventor cut off a small piece, put it in a groove between two clamps of iron and placed the latter in the furnace. The satisfactory light obtained from the tarred lampblack had convinced him that filaments of carbon of a texture not previously used in electric lighting were the hidden agents to make a thorough success of incandescent lighting, and it was with this view that he sought to test the carbon remains of a cotton thread. At the expiration of an hour he removed the iron mold containing the thread from the furnace and took out the delicate carbon framework of the thread—all that was left of it after its fiery ordeal. This slender filament he placed in a globe and connected it with the wires leading to the machine generating the electric current. Then he extracted the air from the globe and turned on the electricity.

Presto! A beautiful light greeted his eyes. He turns on more current expecting the fragile filament instantly to fuse; but no, the only change is more brilliant light. He turns on more current, and still more, but the delicate thread remains entire. Then, with characteristic impetuosity and wondering and marveling at the strength of the little filament, he turns on the full power of his machine and eagerly watches the consequence. For a minute or more the tender little thread seems to struggle with the intense heat passing through it—

Upton's Cartoon Bulb: Banking on Tech Stocks Francis Upton and other Menlo Park insiders watched the financial speculation over Edison's electrical work with gleeful anticipation. Many were small stockholders in the Edison companies and stood to make a lot of money. Some went on to manage metropolitan illuminating companies of their own.
Courtesy of the Edison National Historical Site, National Park Service, U.S. Department of the Interior.

heat that would melt the diamond itself—then at last it succumbs and all is darkness. The powerful current had broken it in twain, but not before it had emitted a light of several gas jets. Eagerly the inventor hastened to examine under the microscope this curious filament, apparently so delicate, but in reality much more infusible than platinum, so long considered one of the most infusible of metals. The microscope showed the surface of the filament to be highly polished and its parts interwoven with each other.

THE PAPER LIGHT

It was also noticed that the filament had obtained a remarkable degree of hardness compared with its fragile character before it was subjected to the action of the current. Night and day, with scarcely rest enough to eat a hearty meal or catch a brief repose, the inventor kept up his experiments, and from carbonizing pieces of thread he went to splinters of wood, straw, paper and many other substances never before used for that purpose. The results of his experimentation showed that the substance best adapted for carbonization and the giving out of incandescent light was paper preferably thick like cardboard, but giving good results even when very thin. The beautiful character of the illumination and the steadiness, reliability and non-fusibility of the carbon filament were not the only elements incident to the new discovery that brought joy to the heart of Edison. There was a further element—not the less necessary because of its being hidden—the element of a proper and uniform resistance to the passage of the electric current...

THE GENERATING MACHINE

Mr. Edison's first experiments in machines for generating the electric current did not meet with success. His primal apparatus was in the form of a large tuning fork, constructed in such a way that its ends vibrated with great rapidity before the poles of a large magnet. These vibrations could be produced with comparatively little power. Several weeks of practice proved, however, that the machine was not practical, and it was laid aside. Then followed a number of other forms, leading up gradually to the one at present used. Bearing in mind the principle common to all magneto-electric machines—viz., that the current is produced by the rotation of magnets near each other—it will not be difficult to understand in a general way, how his machine operates. . . .

THE ELECTROMETER

The apparatus for measuring the amount of electricity used by each householder is a simple contrivance consisting of an electrolytic cell and a small coil of wire, appropriately arranged in a box, the latter being about half the size of an ordinary gas meter, and like a gas meter it can be placed in any part of the house. The measurement is obtained by the deposit of copper particles on a little plate in the electrolytic cell, such deposit being caused by the electric current passing through the cell. At the end of any period, say one month, the plate is taken by the inspector to the central office, where the copper deposit is weighted and the amount of electricity consumed determined by a simple calculation. . . .

EDISON'S ASSISTANTS

Before concluding this article it is only proper that due credit should be given to those whose untiring energy and skilled handicraft made possible the perfection of the great inventor's system—viz. his chief laboratory assistants; for although Edison's was the mind that originated all, theirs were the hands that deftly carried out his wishes.

Principal among his assistants, and so intimately associated with him in his work that his absence from the laboratory is invariably a signal for Mr. Edison to suspend labor, is Mr. Charles Batchelor. For the past eight years Mr. Batchelor has worked side by side with the inventor, carrying out his plans with rare ability, and to his energy and skill is due not a little. Next come Messrs. Upton and Kruesi, both heads of departments, the one attending to the fine electrical work and the other to the mechanical details of the machine department. Among the others whose ability has helped to contribute to the inventor's great success, each in his particular sphere, are Mr. Griffin, Mr. Carman, Mr. Jehl, Mr. Force and Mr. Boehm.

A Fan Letter

February 1880

This document is one example of the many thousands of unsolicited letters Edison received throughout his career from individuals seeking to do business with him in one way or another. Letter writers often mentioned newspaper accounts as their impetus for writing, and their memories of what they read often seem to have been at least as unreliable as the press itself. The word "perpetual" in this letter taps a long tradition of amateur speculation about perpetual motion machines, though here it is modified paradoxically as electrically perpetual.

NEW YORK, FEBRUARY 1880

Dear Sir:

Some 3 months ago I read in the N.Y. Herald a short notice about an electric perpetual fan of your invention, which you would exhibit in the spring. Benefactor as you have long grown to humanity, this invention would be another link to your glory. I judge that a perpetual fan must be the most pleasant thing that ever could be bestowed upon heat-oppressed humanity. Particularly will it be a blessing to us of the South. I intend shortly to return there and if I could introduce this article there I think I should be able to dispose of 50,000 such fans in different cities of the South during spring & summer, providing the cost of the same is not too high. Should you honor me with your kind reply I should beg to ask the following questions. What may be the cost of one ordinary size outfit with fan? Have there been any applications from the South before mine? Can I hope to be instrumental in introducing this invention in the South? When & where could I see you on your next sojourn in New York?

Awaiting your kind reply, I remain, Sir, yours Respectfully,

L. Marx
223 East Broadway

Boehm v. Edison:
Two Versions of Invention at Menlo Park
August–October 1881

When two parties apply for a patent on the same invention, the U.S. government declares an "Interference," and holds legal proceedings to determine whose invention it really is. In this case, Ludwig Boehm [sometimes spelled Bohm] claimed to have invented the vacuum pump, which successfully exhausted air from Edison's incandescent bulbs. Boehm was a somewhat disgruntled alumnus of Menlo Park, who had worked for Edison in 1879 and 1880 and suffered many practical jokes at the hands of his coworkers. For his part, Edison claimed that the vacuum pump was his invention, made in the regular course of trials and errors at his laboratory. Edison marshaled a lot more evidence than Boehm to support his version of events, including testimony by Boehm's former coworkers. The interference was declared in the fall of 1880, and this testimony (Q and A) with cross-examinations (X-Q and A) was compiled in August 1881. The Patent Office decided in Edison's favor in October 1881, but Boehm's version of the way Menlo Park worked is far from implausible.

Boehm's Version

Q.1. What is your name, residence, and occupation?

A. My name is Ludwig K. Boehm. I live at 123 Second Avenue in New York City; I am twenty-two years old; I am an Electrician, employed by the American Electric Light Company.

Q.2. Please state where you were employed at the time when the invention, forming the subject of this interference, was made?

A. I was employed in Menlo Park, at the laboratory of Mr. Thomas A. Edison, in the special capacity of making experimental apparatus appertaining to incandescent lighting.

Q.3.   What special kind of apparatus did you make?

A.   I made first experimental lamps with platinum spirals as light-giving agents, and also vacuum apparatus, or air-pumps, for exhausting those experimental bulbs. . . .

Q. 23.   How long did you stay in the employ of Mr. Edison, and when did you leave him?

A.   I stayed with him about fourteen months, and left towards the end of October 1880.

Q.24.   Did he during the time you were employed with Mr. Edison, suggest this Improvement in Vacuum pumps, the subject matter of this Interference; or did he ever give you instructions to make it?

A.   No sir, he never did.

Q.25.   What was the reason, when you made the application for a patent, to take this step, or what induced you to apply for a patent?

A.   I thought I would get a compensation in the shape of a permanent position from Mr. Edison; besides this, Mr. Edison wanted to take contracts with the Edison Electric Light Company, which I should carry out, the profits being divided between us; when I saw my expectations were not to be fulfilled, I left Mr. Edison and applied for my patent. . . .

X-Q.32.   When did you come to this country?

A.   I landed about the middle of September, 1878.

X-Q.33.   Was your trade that of a glass-blower?

A.   I was, as I have said, a pupil of Dr. Geissler, who was a physicist, . . . I tried to obtain knowledge, theoretical as well as practical, and became regarded as a skillful glass-blower of philosophical instruments. . . . My trade was partly glass-blowing.

X-Q.34.   When you went to work for Mr. Edison, in what building did you work?

A.   For the first days I worked on the first floor of the laboratory building, then I worked in a small cottage, which had been used before for taking photographs, near the laboratory building. I stayed in here for about a year; then I was ordered to the lamp factory on the second floor, and I stayed there until I left Mr. Edison's employ. . . .

X.Q.37.   Who worked in the same room with you while you were working in the laboratory building?

A.   Generally Frank Upton, a mathematician, and there were present generally assistants of Edison—Chas. Batchelor, Martin Force, Francis Jehl and other men. . . .

X-Q. 46.   When you made the experimental lamps, did you make them under the direction of Mr. Edison or some one of his assistants?

A. ... Mr. Edison and Mr. Batchelor suggested a great many things, assistants suggested, everybody suggested; I myself suggested and carried out the suggestions; I kept memoranda of all those suggestions, orders and devices.

X-Q.47. What became of these memoranda books?

A. They were in Mr. Edison's possession when I left. . . .

X-Q.63. Was it the habit of Mr. Edison to bring or send to you sketches of the constructions he wished to have made in glass?

A. Partly he sent sketches or messages, partly he came in himself, instructing me, sometimes making drawings in those memorandum books; many times he conversed with me about ways how things could be improved, and several times he said—"use your brains.". . .

X-Q.90. When you left the employment of Mr. Edison, in whose employ did you go?

A. I went in the employ of Mr. Maxim, or the United States Electric Light Company.

X-Q.91. What inducements did you hold out to Mr. Maxim or his company for your employment?

A. I told them that I had been a pupil of Dr. Geissler and an assistant of Mr. Edison in incandescent lighting, having been employed by the latter in experimental work on incandescent lamps and vacuum apparatus.

Edison's Version

Q.1. Please state your name, age, residence and occupation.

A. Thomas A. Edison; age 34; residence Menlo Park, N.J.; occupation inventor.

Q.2. The issue in this interference, as defined by the Patent Office, is "In a Sprengel air pump the mercury supply tube having formed integral therewith a contraction above the fall tube for regulating the flow of mercury." Did you make this invention; if so, when and where, and under what circumstances?

A. If there be any invention I made the same some time in March or April, 1879, at my laboratory at Menlo Park. The pump [described] was made by [another] glass blower named Baetz at the time stated. The circumstances under which it was made were that I was endeavoring to obtain a mercury pump for obtaining high vacua in the bulbs of my electric lamps, and a great number of different pumps of different forms and constructions were made by Mr. Baetz for me about the time mentioned. . . .

Q.7. Were the Sprengle pumps [modified as described] made by Mr. Baetz for you before Mr. Ludwig K. Boehm came to Menlo Park?

A. Yes, sir.

Q.8. Were such pumps put in practical use for exhausting air from electric lamps before Mr. Boehm came to Menlo Park?

A. Yes, sir.

Q.9. Please state under what circumstances and in what capacity Mr. Boehm was employed by you?

A. Desiring the services at all times, night and day, of a glass blower, I advertised for one. Mr. Boehm came in answer to the advertisement, stating that he was a practical glass blower, and he showed me a thermometer which he had made, stating that he was working for some firm in New York making such thermometers. I asked him if he desired work, and the wages he required, and if he could make vacuum pumps. He stated that he did desire work; that he could make pumps, and wanted twenty dollars a week, which I agreed to give him, and he continued as a glass blower in my employ until he left me.

Q.10. Do you remember about what time it was when he entered your employ?

A. Some time in August 1879.

Q.11. From whom was Mr. Boehm to take directions in regard to the work he should do?

A. From me, generally, and also from my assistants, who practically worked the pumps and discovered the defects and advantages [of them in trying to make light bulbs].

Q.12. Was Boehm an electrician as well as a glass blower?

A. I never knew that he was.

Q.13. What degree of inventive capacity did he display in conferences with you while in your employ?

A. I never knew him to invent anything. . . .

Q.15. How close was your supervision of Mr. Boehm's work, and how frequently did you overlook it during the time he was in your employ?

A. My supervision was very close. I was always on hand; every change was known by me, and I had modifications which I desired made, so numerous that Boehm was unable to make one-tenth part of such changes. He was kept busy repairing pumps, making new pumps and lamps, from fifteen to twenty hours each day. I probably saw him ten times a day.

Draft Report for Investors

September 1881

By 1881 Edison and his associates were struggling to exploit the new technology. Demonstrations and exhibitions of the Edison system continued in the United States and Europe, while the original Edison Electric Light Company was quickly joined by half a dozen companies. These companies were organized to manufacture everything from light bulbs (Edison Lamp Works, 1880), lighting fixtures and sockets (Bergman & Company, 1881) to underground conduits for burying wires (Electric Tube Company, 1881). Other companies were formed to build individual, isolated lighting plants, or to construct central power stations. Investors were curious and in many cases willing. Some companies remained partnerships under the control of Edison and his close associates, while others required larger infusions of capital and a broader pool of investors. Edison's friend Edward H. Johnson was a partner in Bergman & Co. and the Edison Lamp Works (eventually the Edison Lamp Company, 1881). He drafted the following report.

EDISON ELECTRIC LIGHT STOCK CONSIDERED AS A SPECULATIVE HOLDING FOR THE ENSUING QUARTER

By Edward H. Johnson

In the fall of 1878 Thomas A. Edison made the assertion to a newspaper reporter that he was about to enter the Electric Light field of exploration and felt confident that he had found the true solution of the great problem . . . the sub-division of the Electric Current and its distribution among innumerable points over large areas from a common source of supply. The great reputation which Mr. Edison had just made by the invention of the Phonograph carrying his name as it did from without the smaller circle of the professional to the larger one of the non-professional caused his announcement to have an effect which he could not have anticipated. . . . The latter and much larger circle read these same reports with blind confidence in the inventor of the

Phonograph. Hence it became the almost universal belief that the whole problem was solved and it was fully anticipated that within a space of two or three months at least Mr. Edison's light would be seen everywhere and gas would utterly disappear to be known no more forever.

The newspapers were of course eager to feed this sensation as they would any other which lent interest to their columns. Hundreds of interviews were made up in the Editorial rooms and in the private sanctuaries of that Great American Institution the "Reporter" having no other basis than a vivid imagination. . . . The effect of this was to place Mr. Edison in a false and embarrassing position. Well knowing however that he had found the true principle of accomplishing the work and thus ultimately justifying all that had been so prematurely claimed for him and confident in his ability to perform an immense amount of labor in an incredible short time, he gainsaid nothing but went earnestly to work to evolve from out [of] the chaos of the unknown the order and proportion requisite to put his ideas into practical shape. . . . Mr. Edison made the error, and has continued to make it in all allusions to the time when his work will be finally finished, in assuming that the difficulty of the moment was the sole one, and it surmounted the work was done. This error, not of judgment so much as of a desire to quell the rising disquietude of the public and his friends, is the only one he has made. In the matter of his work he has absolutely made none. . . .

A considerable disappointment and a consequent reaction of the popular mind had been the resultant factor in all this and now we find a lack of confidence almost as universal as the earlier confidence and having even less foundation for its existence.

Thus when Mr. Edison finally made a demonstration at Menlo Park in December 1879, although on a scale of comparative magnitude, it fell short of conviction and his demonstration consisting of 700 lamps supplied from one source and distributed over an area of one mile square, fed by an aggregate of 8 miles of underground wires and supplying all the light used in the factories, stores, dwellings, shops &c. within the compass of this mile, was still looked upon as simply a Laboratory Experiment. From this it became apparent that the thing must be put into practical operation on the premises of the public where all the world could see for themselves. The Menlo Park Exhibit was thereupon promptly abandoned, Mr. Edison and his entire corps of assistants and workmen coming to New York and immediately inaugurating steps to establish his system here on a scale which will absolutely and permanently displace gas and other artificial lights from a densely populated district of the city. One mile square this work is rapidly drawing to completion.

The object of this paper is to plainly state the facts in such a way as to enable the reader to form a judgment as to the result upon the public mind and consequently upon the stock of the Edison Companies of the final opening up to the public gaze and use of the large district. . . . Will the public accept the problem as solved and seek investment in the Edison stocks?

EDISON'S SYSTEM

Edison early determined to follow a certain course in order to the sooner reach complete success which was at great variance with that pursued by other inventors. He has, as it transpires, wisely adhered to his line of procedure in spite of strong opposition from within and without his own immediate associates. Chief among the things resolved upon were the following:

First. That the true and only method of an indefinite subdivision and distribution of the Electric Light was what is known as the "Incandescent" principle. All previous attempts had been made on the "Arc" principle and all such efforts have as yet proven absolute failures.

Second. That to create a successful rival, commercially, [to] Gas lighting, [an] electric system must be on the same scale and as simple and practicable in all its details. Otherwise its supervision would entail fatal costs and annoyance and that in consequence the electricity must be generated off the premises of the consumer and sent to it through the streets as in the case of gas. This has been pronounced impossible for the three following reasons,

That a small constant and steady light requiring only the attention of ordinary domestic servants could not be produced.

That if such a lamp was produced the amount of copper for supplying a vast number of them from a common source of supply would be so vast as to swamp the enterprise by the investment in copper alone.

That further, an electrical generator of sufficient capacity to render such general lighting practicable could not be successfully operated for the reason that so great an amount of electricity could not be controlled. "It would be irresistible as a thunderbolt."

All three of these impossibilities have become so generally accepted as actualities that it is scarcely worth recalling the earlier prophecies except to illustrate the magnitude of the work Edison has accomplished by the negative evidence they offer.

Third. That his only rival in a commercial sense would be the Gas interest—that in consequence his constant aim should be to attain in every department of his work the highest possible economical mien rather than the greatest maximum capacity. . . .

Fourth. That he would not allow any side issues to distract his time, attention and energy or that of his establishment from the main work in hand: In consequence of this he has up to the present date absolutely declined all propositions however tempting to engage in what might be termed "Isolated" lighting—that is lighting with small individual machines. He has resolutely refused to inaugurate the legal steps requisite to enforce the rights granted by his patents notwithstanding that many audacious infringements of his patents are being made.

The wisdom of this course was at first disputed by his associates, but is now fully recognized since by virtue of it he has doubly fortified himself against successful competition. His system is already so complete in every detail of practical and commercial importance that were his patents to offer him no protection what[so]ever he would still be absolutely alone in the field of real competition with gas—none other having so much as contemplated the work of Electric Lighting on a sufficiently comprehensive basis as to render them worthy of the attention of the gas interest. It would in fact require years for them unitedly to reach the stage now occupied by Edison, ere which time he would of course be proportionately advanced. It is not too much to say that if a combination of all other inventors and their product could be effected they would still be unable to do what Mr. Edison is now doing, and this aside from all questions of patents they would simply be physically unequal to the task from a lack of comprehension of the essentials. This belief is founded upon the knowledge of the obstacles Mr. Edison has overcome in rendering the three several "Impossibilities" accomplished facts, and it explains why all the so called rivals are so unanimous in proclaiming what Mr. Edison has done "impossible of accomplishment." Others to reach the same end would have to travel over the same ground and Mr. Edison has made it a point while publishing broadcast the ends attained to leave no traces of the paths he has pursued, and since no combination or aggregation of Mediocrity ever did or ever can equal in fertility of resource the single brain of genius he is not to be overtaken so long as he lives. This is his determination and will prove to be the final issue. By preserving secrecy as to the means of accomplishing the various ends Mr. Edison has rapidly entrenched himself in an absolute monopoly without educating others to the point of following him closely or anticipating him in the Patent Office. This he has been enabled to do by filing his applications for Patents and allowing them to remain unissued in the Patent Office to the full period provided by law during all which time he is of course constantly adding to or emending them as his experiments may suggest. Thus when they finally issue they are comprehensive and cover the ground broadly and completely forestall all claims of priority. Were Edison to appear in court at any time prior to the issue of his final Patents he would be compelled to show his hand fully. This would be a great disadvantage as there is no educator in scientific work equal to a legal contest over an invention. Every detail is expounded with such clearness as to be easily comprehended and naturally becomes full of suggestion to investigators. When Mr. Edison does enter the courts it will be to show an invulnerability never before attained where so many or so valuable patents were concerned. No invention of any age has been so systematically or so thoroughly protected by a close study and application of the patent law as has this of Mr. Edison's.

He has woven a web so compact that were it to be perforated in a hundred places it would still be an effective defense. The controlling features are already secured, so that Mr. Edison alone can operate a general system. Others even at the utmost can only do petty work in an isolated way.

THE EDISON UNDERTAKING

The Edison Company are now engaged in preparing their 1st district in New York City. It is comprised within the following boundaries—Wall St.—South Spruce St.—North Nassau St.—West and the East River, East and has within its borders 1500 Gas Consumers, using upwards of 20,000 gas jets, each and every one of which it is proposed to supplant with an electric jet, or lamp. 1100 of these gas consumers have already signed contracts for the Edison Light and will require from 15 to 17000 lamps. Their promises have already been "wired" for these lamps and they only await the delivery of the electricity at their doors. This is to be effected as follows.

THE SYSTEM

The plan is to establish a central station or source of supply fitted up with the requisite Electrical Generators and distribute the electricity therefrom through conductors encased in Iron Pipes and laid underground to each and every consumer within the district. These conductors will be tapped by service conductors at each house and the electricity delivered through an Electrical Meter, precisely as in the case of gas. No other apparatus will be on the Consumer's premises than the meter and the lamps.

Existing gas fixtures are being utilized for supporting the electric lamps, without interfering with the use of the gas, or detracting from the ornamental character of the fixture. Thus the consumer will have either gas or electricity between which he can make his own comparisons as to cost, quality &c. &c., or he may use both at one and the same time. Special care has been taken to provide for this in order that the comparison which Mr. Edison courts may be made public themselves. The consumer pays for the wiring and for the fixture attachments just as he does for gas pipe fixtures, but the lamps are supplied free of cost. They cost so little and they last so long that it has been decided to charge them up to the cost of producing the electricity, which can be done, and the light be sold still for less than gas. The consumer therefore pays so much per "thousand" for his light. The amount he uses being recorded by the meter.

PRESENT CONDITION OF THE WORK

The Central Station.　Two buildings, Nos. ____ Pearl St., have been secured and the work of fitting them for the reception of the machinery is well under way. It is fully expected they will be ready for occupation by November or December of this year [1881].

The Central Station plant will consist of about 12 steam dynamo machines of 125 horse power each, with ample boiler capacity for producing the steam. There will be devices for regulating the electrical pressure for the entire district and means and methods employed for an absolute guarantee of the reliability of the Light at all times.

... The boilers and steam engines for this station have been contracted for and are deliverable Oct. 1st to 15th. ... These machines are three fold the largest electrical machines in the World. ...

The Underground Conductors.   The manufacture of these "Tubes" is being prosecuted rapidly at the shops of the Edison Tube Works 65 Washington St. N.Y. They will be ready in ample time and will be laid at the rate of one mile per day. The work of laying them will shortly begin. These conductors consist of two half round copper rods kept apart by insulating washers, the whole then slipped into a wrought iron pipe and the interstices filled with an insulating compound of Mr. Edison's invention in liquid form which afterwards congealing leaves the whole a solid mass capable of being bent and twisted without injury to the copper or the insulation.

Meters.   The work of manufacturing the meters though not in so forward a state as that of the other branches is still progressing satisfactorily. They will be ready ere the station is in operation.

Fixtures.   These are being made of every conceivable style and pattern both electrical in their entirety and partially electrical and partially gas. Also innumerable forms of attachments wherewith to affix the lamps to existing gas fixtures so as to obviate the expense to the consumer of new fixtures. Messrs. Bergmann & Co. 108 Wooster St. N.Y. have the exclusive manufacture of appliances for [this] department and they have a large establishment employing 100 skilled mechanics and have already a large stock of goods on hand to meet the demand which will be created by the opening of the district station. The Edison Electric Lamp Co. at Menlo Park, N.J. and at East Newark, N.J. have been in operation for over a year and have in stock many times more lamps than will be required by the first district. The New factory at East Newark is being fitted up to give it a capacity of 50,000 lamps per day.

Wire Running.   The running of the wires from the meter to each and every burner of lamp to be used by the 1100 subscribers of the 1st district being a matter requiring a considerable amount of time the work was begun some four months since and being prosecuted by a gang of 100 wire-men under competent supervision is now practically complete.

. . . Thus it is seen that all reaches of this gigantic undertaking are rapidly approaching completion. The Central Station plant, the street conductors, the . . . appliances and the lamps are one and all practically receiving their final touches and the long siege of experimental work by which they have been evolved from the chaos found by Mr. Edison is at an end. Every detail has now successfully run the gamut of actual trial and success final and overwhelming is as certain as to-morrow's sun. True there may be some minor hitches incidental to the first starting of so vast a plant, but as every single component of that plant has been tested thoroughly with special reference to the work it is ultimately destined to do there can be no serious failures or even delays.

The public is to day in ignorance of the facts above given and is therefore not aware of the real value of the Edison Electric Light Stock. The awakening will come ere another 60 or 90 days have passed. The time to buy is at present.

Mr. Edison has shown his own confidence by the investment of every dollar of his capital and his current revenue derived from other sources in his various works. He has over $100,000 cash in the Lamp Manufacturing Co. and $200,000 cash in the Machine Works besides smaller amounts in the Tube Works and other enterprises connected with the enterprise.

The cost of the installation of the district in New York is borne by The Edison Electric Illuminating Co. of New York, a local organization having no connection with the Edison Electric Light Co., the parent company, except that the chief individual stockholders in the two companies are the same. The Edison Electric Light Co. of New York, the parent Co., is the owner of all the patents for the N.E. and Canada. Its function is to develop the apparatus and then simply to license local organizations throughout the country to use the same. Its output has all been made—henceforth its only expenditures will be such as are involved in defending its patents and maintaining its existence. Its capital stock consists of 4800 shares $100 each $480,000. This is the total present capitalization of an electric lighting system and is now a formidable rival to the $80,000,000 invested in Gas. The stock is now selling at $1000 per share, that is 4800 shares—$4,800,000.

ESTIMATED VALUATION

... I have shown how Mr. Edison first excited the hopes and the cupidity of the public by a mere assertion of what he proposed to do. Now I show what he has done toward their realization, and that the public are in the dark as to the nearness of the final issue as well as of its completeness. The question is what will be the effect upon his stock when the newspapers announce the successful opening up of the New York district with its thousands of lights ...

If it rose as it did ... on his promise what will it go to on the fulfillment of that promise? This work will rank with the creation of the Telegraph, the Steam Engine, or the Printing Press, and would have taken the same number of years to perfect it but for the colossal brain, untiring energy and vast resources of the greatest inventor of this or any other age. To day the Edison Electric Light is popularly believed to be a failure; to-morrow its success will be recognized the World over.

Notice from the Edison Company for Isolated Lighting
November 1885

Inventing and installing an electrical system was one thing, but selling it was altogether another. This notice is from the Edison Company for Isolated Lighting's Bulletin for Agents. It shows some of the arguments made for incandescent lighting and hints at the slow initial progress of electrification. Enthusiasm ran well ahead of electrification in most places.[1] Nor were the benefits of domestic electrification immediately apparent to everyone: as late as 1902 the American novelist Edith Wharton wrote that "Nothing has done more to vulgarize interior decoration than the general use of gas and of electricity in the living-rooms of modern houses. Electric light especially, with its harsh white glare, which no expedients have as yet overcome, has taken from our drawing-rooms all air of privacy and distinction"!

The Most Perfect System of Electric Lighting Is the Edison Incandescent Light. It Presents the Following Unequaled Advantages.

It is the most economical artificial light.
It is brighter than gas.
It is steady as sunlight—never flickers.
It is reliable.
It emits no heat.

---

[1] At the turn of the twentieth century there were still only 3,620 central stations in the United States, producing a total of 2.3 billion kilowatt hours a year. (Single power stations can produce more than that today.) Many Americans living in small farming communities would have to wait until the 1930s for rural electrification.

It cannot vitiate the air.

It gives no disagreeable odor.

It is beneficial to the eyesight—not injurious, as gas.

It is the most beautiful light known.

It is perfectly safe.

It cannot produce fire in the most inflammable substance.

It cannot explode.

It cannot produce death by poison, as gas often does.

It cannot cause a hurtful shock to the human system, as the arc lights do.

It gives colors their natural tints.

It can be placed in any desired position, thus utilizing all the rays of light.

It secures (by use of small sixteen-candle power lamps) uniform and economical distribution of the light—impossible with arc lights of large power.

It can be used anywhere, under any conditions.

It cannot flare or be blown out by the wind.

It dispenses entirely with matches or special lighting apparatus.

It is perfectly under control. Each lamp is independent of the others, yet all or any desired number can be lighted or extinguished instantaneously, so that—

It is a perfect burglar-alarm.

It does not consume Oxygen, and thereby exhaust the atmosphere of an apartment.

It produces no poisonous product of combustion, such as carbonic acid, or carbonic oxide, which are both largely produced by gas and oil lights.

It produces no water of combustion. A gas or oil light produces a large quantity of water in an evening, sufficient, if condensed, to partly fill a tumbler.

The electric conductors contain no poisonous, bad-smelling substance to escape in the house, through defective joints, and to cost the consumer an outlay for medical attendance, and a steady running expenditure, more or less, for leakage.

It does not emit smoke to blacken the ceilings or walls, or destroy pictures by covering them with a layer of oily soot, which cannot be cleaned off.

It does not leak sulphurated hydrogen to blacken silverware, or lead-painted woodwork, or destroy oil paintings.

It cannot, like gas, be improperly extinguished, and pour a dangerous vapor into the apartment for hours, which may destroy the sleeping customer by poison, or a violent explosion.

It is the only system complete in all its details, and which can guarantee throughout the validity of its patents.

4

Modern Living

The documents in this chapter register American attitudes toward progress at the same time they help to identify the many and elaborate ways in which life seemed newly modern at the end of the nineteenth century and the beginning of the twentieth. A popular song in 1890 forecast,

> If Edison is still alive
>   In 1892,
> Electric horses we shall drive
>   In 1892.
> Electric dinners we shall eat.
> Electric brooms will clean the street.
> Police will have electric feet
> In 1892.[1]

The verse suggests the optimism with which electrification was promoted and received in the United States. But enthusiasm did not proceed unabated: There was an economic downturn, or "panic," in 1893. Banks closed and businesses failed. Nor were the specific features of progress inevitable. The published accounts, personal correspondence, and trade promotions included in this chapter together render a more complicated sense of modernity. Groups of documents address an array of technologies with which Edison was associated and which together helped to shape individual and collective experiences of their day. Selections regarding new media like motion pictures and musical phonographs suggest the emergence of mass markets and modern patterns of leisure. Selections regarding transportation, housing, and politics equally suggest new experiences of public space and public life.

---

[1] From "In 1892" by Matt C. Woodward (Willis Woodward Co., 1890).

Phonographs and the Function
of Recorded Sound in Transition

Edison returned to and "perfected" (so he announced) his phonograph in 1887–88. Like everyone else, he envisioned a variety of applications for recorded sound at its inception. Inventors, investors, manufacturers, and, soon, record producers all gambled over the future of recorded sound. Testing, creating, and trying to sustain consumers' desire for phonographic devices meant defining the place of the new technology in the world and everyday life. In 1890 the primary function of the phonograph was still thought by many to be secretarial; the North American Phonograph Company bought the rights from Edison to lease dictation phonographs to business offices throughout the country. Gradually, however, the success of "nickel-in-the-slot" phonographs corrected such assumptions and showed that entertainment records could be a serious business, and a very lucrative one. When home phonographs eventually replaced the nickel-in-the-slot trade, listening to records put traditional practices of home music making in jeopardy. As bandleader John Philip Sousa recognized in an article entitled "The Menace of Mechanical Music" (1906), listening to music was becoming a passive activity, and a woman's ability to play competently on a piano would soon cease to signify middle-class aspiration or gentility. The after-dinner sing-along was doomed. "What of the national throat?" Sousa asked; "Will it not weaken? What of the national chest? Will it not shrink?"

TALKING DOLLS: NEWS ITEMS AND ANECDOTES (1890–1892)

Scientific American, April 26, 1890

EDISON'S PHONOGRAPHIC DOLL

The new "talking doll industry" established upon the basis of the Edison phonograph, has reached such importance as to entitle it to more than a passing notice.... The finished doll ... has the same appearance as other dolls; but its body is made of tin and the interior thereof is filled with a mechanism very much like that of the commercial phonograph, but of course much more simple and inexpensive. The cylinder of the phonograph ... is mounted on a sleeve which slides upon the shaft, the sleeve being screw-threaded so as to cause the cylinder to move lengthwise in the shaft. . . . The cylinder carries a ring of wax-like material, upon which is recorded the speech or song to be repeated by the doll . . . The funnel at the top of the phonographic apparatus opens underneath the breast of the doll, which is perforated to permit the sound to escape. By the simple operation of turning the crank any child can make the doll say "Mary had a little lamb," "Jack and Jill," or whatever it was, so to speak, taught to say in the phonograph factory.

Philadelphia Times, January 2, 1891

A BOOM THAT COLLAPSED

COMPLETE FAILURE OF THE MUCH-HERALDED PHONOGRAPHIC DOLL

WHY EDISON DREW OUT OF IT

The most striking feature of the trade in toys during the holiday season just closed has been the complete collapse of the so-called Edison phonographic dolls from which so much was expected. Their manufacture has been stopped and Mr. Edison has forbidden the future use of his name by the company which made them and with which he had only a nominal connection. And thus the fond dream of many a little maid who has looked forward to some day owning a dolly which could lisp "Mary had a little lamb" will be rudely shattered. Leading dealers in toys and novelties inform me that the phonographic dolls were all made in Germany, and that the stories about little girls gathering in Edison's work rooms at Menlo Park and talking to the little cylinders which were afterwards to form the "innards" of countless dolls were all manufactured tales intended to arouse public interest in the new novelty. I know myself that the manager of the new enterprise gave newspaper writers warm invitations to inspect the making of the wonder manikins, but he invariably failed to fix a day, on the plea that "some minor details still remain to be perfected."

Its proprietors were confident that an enormous fortune awaited them. The first doll made was presented in Vienna to Princess Elizabeth, granddaughter of the Emperor Francis Joseph, and this fact was heralded by cable from the Austrian capital. . . . The new company prepared for a big boom and secured a really magnificent suite of show rooms on Fifth Avenue, near Twentieth Street [in New York City]. . . . Orders for dolls actually poured in from toy dealers all over the country, and it was found impossible to satisfy their demand. One store alone in New York sold 800 at prices ranging from $10 to $25, according to the style of dress, and the proprietor told me he could have easily disposed of 3,000 if he could have obtained them. All this was well and good until the dolls reached their destination and were put to the test of their vocal powers. Then the trouble began.

Of course, sensible people anticipate that the phonographic doll could, at the best, prove but a fragile toy, as the delicate machinery might clearly recite, "Now I lay me down to sleep," in a toy shop, would be liable to refuse to do so after baby had tried its powers for the five hundredth time on Christmas Day. But worse than this happened. Dolls which did their duty in the store, after being transported by express or delivery wagon, when summoned to do their tasks for the first time after purchase, emitted nothing but unintelligible and discordant squeaks. One dealer out of the first 200 phonographic dolls he sold, had 188 returned, and after that warned all buyers that they took them at their own risk. Notwithstanding this, many people insisted on having them.

Examination revealed the fact that the faithless dolls could not even be repaired. Handling and transportation almost invariably disarranged the delicate needle from the almost invisible paraffin groves, its passage through which reproduces the sound waves. It was found impossible to remedy this defect. Mr. Edison, upon learning of this, insisted that the company had not kept the terms of its compact and demanded that his name should no longer [be] used in connection with the dolls. The new corporation thereupon gave up the struggle in despair and stopped the manufacture of what toy dealers expected to be the greatest novelty ever seen in their business.

New York Morning Advertiser, **March 14, 1892**

EDISON RAID ON AFRICA

SI HASSAN ARMED WITH PHONOGRAPH AND TALKING DOLL

... Si Hassan Den Ali obtained a valuable concession from the World's Fair Committee for the establishment of a Moorish village during the fair and a combined African show. When he went abroad a few months ago he took with him, among other things with which to startle and amuse the natives of Africa, a complete telephone outfit, a phonograph loaded with the popular airs of the day, Negro dialects, speeches and brass band and banjo recitations, a powerful electric battery, several of Edison's talking dolls, and an outfit for sinking artesian wells. ...

... He thought he could win them over by these peaceful demonstrations which would appear to them all-powerful.... From all accounts the explorer is actually demonstrating that the phonograph is more powerful than a Krupp gun. When last heard of Si Hassan was at the Court of Moulay El Hassen. Before exhibiting the inventions he made a speech in which he said he was an envoy from Allah sent to do good among the people of Africa. Then he trotted out the phonograph. When the natives heard a German band give a rendition of "Annie Rooney" and "Mary, Take a Wash," they fell back in awe.... When the talking dolls were produced, the excitement of the natives intensified.... The savages regarded the dolls as things of life, and, through their interpreter said they resembled small people found on the other side of the Atlas mountains.

NICKEL-IN-THE-SLOT PHONOGRAPHS: NEWS ITEMS, PROMOTION, AND ANECDOTES (1890–1892)

New York Journal, **November 9, 1890**

SONGS FOR A NICKEL

PHONOGRAPH PARTIES THE LATEST FORM OF ENTERTAINMENT

THE VOICES OF GREAT SINGERS AND ACTORS HEARD FOR ONLY FIVE CENTS A GROUP

The very latest form of entertainment in this town of marvels is the nickel-in-the-slot phonograph. Nearly a hundred of these unique instruments have been placed in the reading rooms and lobbies and they are proving to be an almost endless source of amusement and gratification.

Each instrument furnishes but one selection, but each hotel is provided with a new cylinder every day and the interest is practically inexhaustible. The selections range from McGinty to Signor Valance, a protege of Adalina Patti vocally, and from a little German band to Professor Seidle instrumentally. One can hear Joe Jefferson in recitation, or one of Eli Perkins's prose lies and in the voice of the prevaricator, for only the price of a poor cigar.

So popular have the nickel-in-the-slot phonographs become that blasé men about town, who have squeezed all the juice out of the New York amusement lemon, hail it with delight. The ruling fad now among this class of men is the phonograph party. Four or five men start out together from a given hotel to take in all the phonographs they can find. At the Albermarle Hotel they each in turn start the machine with a nickel and listen to a stanza of Fred Warren's latest song. At the Hoffman House they hear Fanny Rice and Jefferson de Angelis . . . and so on, until ten or fifteen hotels have been visited and the party have heard a bit of the very latest things in town rendered with so startling and realistic effect that it seems almost impossible that the human voice can issue from wax and iron.

To give an idea of the variety furnished by these machines it is only necessary to say that $300 worth of music will be furnished by one of them every year. Billy Edwards of the Hoffman House told the writer that the first day the automatic phonograph was placed in that hotel $15 worth of nickels were dropped into the slot. The machines are not sold, but a percentage of the receipts are paid to the proprietor of the hotel or public place in which they are kept.

Prominent singers and readers from all over the country call daily at the headquarters of the company which manufactures the phonograph for the purpose of singing or talking into the funnel which conveys the sound to the wax cylinders upon which the impressions are made. This is voluntary upon the part of these public entertainers, as it furnishes an excellent means of advertising. Each selection is prefaced on the phonograph with a few words as to who the singer or reader is.

The effect on the artist who talks into the machine is peculiar. The oddity lies in the fact of hearing their own voices, a sensation which they have never before enjoyed. . . .

Phonogram, Published by the North American Phonograph Company, 1891

AN IMPORTANT SUGGESTION

It has been suggested that there is danger of too much attention being given by managers of the local [phonograph] companies to the "coin-in-the-slot" device at the expense of the more legitimate business of the companies, of introducing the phonograph into general use among business men [for dictation purposes, in their respective locales]. I have always been of the opinion that the exhibition of the phonograph for amusement purposes was liable to create a wrong impression in the minds of the public as to its actual merits for other purposes.

Nickel-in-the-Slot Phonograph Parlor In the early 1890s patrons could listen to records at public "parlors," where slot machines like these offered two minutes of music for a nickel. Patrons paid for private experiences in public.
Courtesy of the Edison National Historic Site, National Park Service, U.S. Department of the Interior.

The immediate revenue derived from the "coin-in-the-slot" device has been so large as to make this branch of the business very popular among the local companies. I think that it should be controlled by a separate department in each company, leaving the manager and his assistants free to devote their whole attention to the more important work of placing machines.

Too much consideration cannot be given to this suggestion, as upon it is based the ultimate success of the whole enterprise, and those companies who fail to take advantage of every opportunity of pushing the legitimate side of their business, relying only upon the profits derived from the "coin-in-the-slot," will find too late that they have made a fatal mistake.

I think, also, that the "coin-in-the-slot" device is calculated to injure the phonograph in the opinion of those seeing it only in that form, as it has the appearance of being nothing more than a mere toy, and no one would comprehend its value or appreciate its utility as an aid to business men and others for dictation purposes when seeing it only in that form. It therefore behooves all who are interested in its success to counteract the false impression liable to be thus engendered by every means in their power.

HOW IT IS DONE

The [North American Phonograph Company] runs a music factory on an extensive scale at Jersey City, where thousands of fresh airs are turned out on wax [cylinder records] every month. The companies that handle the talking and singing machines in various parts of the country are making some records on their own account, each company having its specialty. For instance, the Washington company is making a specialty, just at present, of band music; the Kentucky company goes in almost exclusively for Negro business—plantation dialogues, with banjo solos interspersed, and scenes on the levee—and so with the others. While the band plays into the great horns, an expert manipulates the [recording] machines. Each phonograph being supplied with a smooth and fresh cylinder of wax, the expert in charge shouts into each horn separately the title of the piece to be played. When he has done this the electric motor is turned on again, the cylinders revolve beneath the recording needles, the band starts up at a signal and the music pours into the big trumpets until each cylinder is as full of sound impressions as it can hold. Then the expert holds up his finger and the band comes to a full stop at the end of the next musical phrase. The full cylinders are taken off the instruments and put aside in pasteboard boxes, and fresh ones are put on. After the title of the next piece has been shouted into each horn, the band starts up again at the signal and the process is repeated. Now and then, if there is a little space left at the end of the cylinders, the band indulges in a wild burst of applause, stamping and shouting in approbation of its own performance. This passes for demonstration by a supposititous audience, of course, when one hears the phonograph reproduce it. All the cylinders are tested before being sold, to make sure they are perfect, about 10 percent of them being rejected as being defective. Selling at from $1 to $2 each, there is a fair profit.

St. Louis Chronicle, February 14, 1891

AUTOMATIC ROBBERS

. . . "That's right, sir. Give it a punch about an inch under the slot. That sort of rattles the nickel into place. You see the incline isn't steep enough to carry the coin down to the machine. By jarring it up you get the machine started. Don't you see?"

"See," yelled the man with the tubes tucked in his ear, "Good God, man, I don't want to see, I want to hear."

The man who is doing the explaining is the bar-tender at the St. James. The man who is swearing is the victim of a phonographic holdup game.

"Do you hear yet? No! O, you'll get it in a second. The song today is the latest. They sang it over at the Standard last week. The name of it is, And You Wink the Other Eye."

"Wink the other eye, eh," asked the listener, resting on the other foot.

"Yes."

"I guess that's what Edison did when he put this thing on the market."

The courteous Job in the apron punched the machine under the slot again, rested his chin on his fist and ear on the glass that covers the machine.

"Ah, there it is! I hear it. I hear it. Don't you?" exclaimed the cocktail artist, raising his head suddenly, knocking the ashes from the victim's cigar and spraying them over his pant leg."

"Yes, I'm beginning to hear it. There's no music about it."

"What does it sound like?"

"Kind of a hissing noise!"

"Guess that's the applause," responded the bartender, making a wild guess. . . . The saloon man hit the machine another belt in the stomach and said with an enticing smile, "You hear the music now, don't you?"

"Hear nothin'. It's a regular buzz-buzz. I guess the fellow must have been in a planing mill when he sang this song. Hang the thing."

Knocking the tubes from his ears, the patient listener deposited an oath with the bartender and went out.

Then the bartender suddenly discovered the machine was out of order.

"Then why didn't you tell him so," said George McManus, of the Grand Opera House.

"Forget it. Why, there's a sign right over the slot, 'out of order today.' But they never see that sign. I never saw a man yet that noticed the 'out of order' sign till after he lost his nickel." "Does it take much swearing to run these phonographs?" asked Mr. McManus. "Ask Chris Von der Ahe. He tried this very phonograph the other day. He told me that it cost him more swearing to run nickel machines than a baseball club. I believed him by the time he got a tune out of this one."

Phonogram, Published by the North American Phonograph Company, 1891

A NEW AUTOMATIC PHONOGRAPH, TO THE TRADE

The Automatic Phonograph Exhibition Co., which controls the patents of the "Nickel-in-the-Slot," is putting out a new machine which is a great improvement over the old one, of which there were about 750 in use from Maine to Montana. . . .

An important feature of the new machine is that plugs, wads, buttons, etc., will not work, and only an exact counterfeit of a nickel in weight and size will operate the phonograph.

The factory is now running night and day to supply new machines in place of the old style. The receipts show no perceptible decrease or increase, but in some special cases, favored by location, some machines pay as much as $24 in one day. The receipts increase or diminish in various machines, as the records, which are changed daily, are good or mediocre. Like a theatrical production, "a good show drawing a full house," and different localities require different attractions.

THE PHONOGRAPH AT HOME: NATIONAL PHONOGRAPH COMPANY ADVERTISEMENTS AND NOTICES (1905–1908)

1905

MR. COLLINS IS NOT A NEGRO.

Possibly because of his great success in singing coon songs and ragtime songs for the Edison Phonograph some people seem to have gained the impression that Arthur Collins is a colored man. Such an impression is naturally amusing to Mr. Collins. It is complimentary, however, to imitate the colored race so closely as to be mistaken for the real article.

1906

When a Man leaves home in the evening it is because he seeks amusement. The best way to keep him home is to give him amusement there. Make home a competitor of downtown, the club, the café, the theatre and the concert hall. No one thing will furnish so much amusement for so many people, so many times, and in so many ways as the Edison Phonograph.

Talk about versatility! If you had a brass band on tap and several leading concert hall singers on salary, and two or three funny men to crack jokes, and a beautiful soprano to sing ballads, you could not give the same amount of varied entertainment that the Edison Phonograph gives by simply changing records.

You can hear the whole program at some nearby store in this town.

1906

EDISON GOLD MOULDED RECORD, NO. 9381.

"Come Down McGinty". . . is an Irish sketch, with orchestra accompaniment, that introduces a new vaudeville team in Campbell and Roberts, who though well known as makers of solo Records have not before sung together. McGinty was at work on a building on a windy day and, being thin, was carried in the air. On his way up his shoes came down and struck McGuire on the head, causing the latter to exclaim: "Come down McGinty, I'll whip you where I'm standing/ Come down McGinty, yes come down from that landing/ I'll whip you, I'll not kick you/ But I'll break your back, you Mick you/ If you come down, come down here McGinty."

1906

EDISON GOLD MOULDED RECORD, NO. 9487.

"Frau Louisa," by the Edison Concert Band, is a composition written by Arthur Pryor, the well-known band master, by whom it is styled a "comedy waltz." The music is characteristic of a German ball where the old style waltz is still popular, and where the modern two-step is unknown. In fact, the music is almost German enough to talk. A few words in German dialect give the Record a unique finish.

1906

When the King of England wants to see a show they bring the show to the castle and he hears it alone in his private theatre. In this country we are all kings as far as having our private show is concerned. We simply buy an Edison Phonograph and listen to the latest popular song, to the famous tenor opera singer, to a fine old hymn, to a ragtime dance or to a funny dialogue. Anything that can be spoken, sung, or played can be reproduced in the Edison Phonograph with great naturalness. If you are a king, why don't you exercise your kingly privilege and have a show of your own in your own house.

Hearing is believing. The dealer will show you.

1907

THOSE FOREIGN RECORDS.

... In a country like this, where so many races are blended, there should be a big market for foreign selections if they were pushed. These Foreign Records are all exceptionally good, being, indeed, the best recorded and most popular in the countries from which they come. There is a great deal of variety among them. Some of the German and French and Grand opera, and some in the lighter vein of the cafe [singer]. They are made by artists well known in their respective countries and deserve recognition as such, not only by French, German or Swedes, as the case may be, but by all Edison Phonograph owners who appreciate good vocal records. About 1,000 Foreign Records are available in the new complete Edison Foreign Selections catalog. They comprise vocal and instrumental numbers in German, French, French-Canadian, Italian, British, Bohemian, Swedish, Polish, Hungarian, Hebrew, Spanish, Holland-Dutch, Danish, Norwegian, Cuban, Mexican, Chinese, Japanese, and a list of South and Central America National Hymns. The vocal Records were made by the foremost native talent, not by foreign-speaking Americans. They are faultlessly recorded and perfect in accent and enunciation. ...

1908

If there is any one class of young men who can appreciate an entertainer like the EDISON PHONOGRAPH it is the college class. Think what it would mean to hear all the new popular songs in your own rooms, whenever you pleased, simply by turning them on.

1908

Don't let the young folks get into the habit of seeking amusement outside of their own homes. It's so easy to give them the best sort of
amusement—clean, hearty, wholesome fun—in their own homes by
means of an Edison Phonograph. It sings the songs they like to hear,
gives them the monologues of clever comedians, plays the music they
are fond of and renders waltzes and two-steps that set their feet
a–tripping.

1908

You needn't be barred from the fun of having an Edison Phonograph
in your home simply because you can't afford to pay for it all at once.
We'll be glad to fix it so that by paying a small amount down you can
have the Phonograph delivered and begin to enjoy it at once, paying
the rest in installments that will be less than it costs you for an
evening's entertainment at the theatre.

1908

[TO OUR DEALERS:] FOREIGN RECORDS SELL.

. . . There is a ready-made demand for the foreign records in every
community. The way to make the most out of it is to first stock the
Records and then make it known that you have done so. The public is
not going to run after any dealer on any article, for the public has
many uses for the hard-earned dollar and isn't anxious to spend it on
anything. A dealer could sell clothing—he could sell groceries, shoes,
pianos, jewelry or anything else if he did not first get the goods on his
floors and then make it known. No; your customers are never going to
force you to put the Foreign Records in—not in a thousand years.
Foreign customers would be the last to think of such a thing. You do
the thinking for them. They are not the recipients of such special
propositions as you have to offer in the songs and instrumental music
of their native land. When they get your suggestion that they can hear
in their own homes their favorite national songs, dances and concert
numbers by leading native artists, it will strike them as a very happy
thought. The proper way to start in is to look around you to find out
what nationalities of foreigners are best represented and order your
records accordingly. . . . When the Records arrive, have some of the
people you are seeking to reach, come in and hear them. Just make a

sale or two and you will find orders for machines and Records will come in thick and fast. Foreigners are clannish, live within a small circle as a rule and keep in close touch with one another. When they get a good thing they pass it along.

1908

BROADWAY VAUDEVILLE ANYWHERE.

On your front porch, for instance, when you are tired with your day's work and lack the energy necessary to entertain yourself. Then the Edison Phonograph will stir you with its marches, amuse you with its rag-time songs and dances or soothe you with its melodies. It sings as sweetly as the most cultivated singer and renders perfectly the tones of the various instruments of orchestras and bands. Perhaps you've heard "talking machines." Have you heard a genuine Edison Phonograph? There's a difference. Some machines merely reproduce sounds and noises. The sweetness and perfect expression for which you prize music are qualities which distinguish the Edison from its imitators.

Electrocution: Original Correspondence and News Items
1887–1888, 1905

The earliest incandescent and arc electric lighting systems needed at least one power generating station for every one-mile radius of electrification. Central stations supplied a direct current (DC) at low voltages, flowing in one direction to the consumer. Then, during the latter half of the 1880s, the fundamentals of electric power distribution were reengineered. Nikola Tesla invented an alternating current (AC) motor, and George Westinghouse put his industrial might behind the distribution of high-voltage AC, which could be transmitted over long distances. Edison resisted the change for a number of reasons, not all of them rational. He authorized experiments and demonstrations in which the electrocution of living beings was meant to prove the dangers of AC. Edison became involved in a gruesome series of experiments in which animals were killed by electricity—dogs, cows, horses, even (as a stunt) an elephant. In conducting these experiments, he also exploited a high-profile public debate about capital punishment as "cruel and unusual" or inhumane, which presaged the first execution by an "electric chair" at a state prison in New York. The chair used alternating current, and Edison apparently wanted the verb "to electrocute" replaced colloquially by the verb "to West-inghouse." Today household electrical current is all of the non-Edison AC type.

A. P. Southwick to Edison, November 8, 1887

Dear Sir,

The commission appointed by the Legislature last year to investigate and report at the coming session the most humane and practical method known to modern science of death in capital cases are desirous of obtaining all the knowledge and facts as to the practicability of using electricity in inflicting capital punishment. Your reputation as a scientist and especially as an electrician has induced me to write you and ask as a favor that you will give me the benefit of your knowledge and opinion in the matter. What would you consider to be the necessary strength of current to produce death with certainty in all cases and under all circumstances? The commission will probably recommend that all executions take place at the State prisons and where there is not an electric plant it will be necessary to have special machines.

What would you recommend as such and what would be the probable expense of the same? In making a report to the Legislature it will be necessary to go into all the particulars of first cost and maintenance &c. If not trespassing upon your time too much I wish you would give me your opinion from a practical standpoint in as elaborate a form as possible that it may be embodied in the coming report. My own opinion has been that a chair constructed for the purpose with metal arms to which the wires were attached passing the current across the chest would be all sufficient.

Hoping to hear from you soon I am Respectfully
Yours A. P. Southwick

A. P. Southwick to Edison, December 5, 1887

Dear Sir:

The question does not arise do we as individuals believe in capital punishment or the right of the Law to kill for certain crimes or that society could not protect itself in some other way but that capital punishment has existed by law in all ages and in all nations and perhaps will for all time to come, this being the fact it appears to me that science and civilization demands some more humane method than the rope. The rope is a relic of barbarism and should be relegated to the past. The reputation you have as an electrician will help as much with the Legislature as Lawmakers in changing the code and it can be done if you and a few others will but assist the commission in their efforts to obtain facts as to the practicability of using electricity. Civilization, science and humanity demand a change, humanity to the living as well as to the unfortunate victim. Hoping you will change your mind on the subject and give us the benefit of your knowledge.

I remain Earnestly
Yours
A. P. Southwick

Edison to A. P. Southwick, December 19, 1887

Dear Sir:

I am in receipt of your letter [of the] 5th instant in further reference to electricity as an agent to supplant the gallows, and have carefully considered your remarks. Your points are well taken and though I would join heartily in an effort to totally abolish capital punishment, I at the same time realize that while the system is recognized by the State, it is the duty of the latter to adopt the most humane method available for the purpose of disposing of criminals under the sentence of death. The best appliance in this connection is to my mind the one which will perform its work in the shortest space of time, and inflict the least amount of suffering upon its victim. This, I believe, can be accomplished by the use of electricity, and the most suitable apparatus for the purpose is that class of dynamo electric machinery, which employs intermittent currents. The most effective of these are known as "alternating machines," manufactured principally in this country by Mr. George Westinghouse, Pittsburgh. . . .

Yours very truly
Thos A Edison

New York Herald, November 1888

SURER THAN ROPE

DEMONSTRATION OF CAPITAL PUNISHMENT BY ELECTRICITY

On January 1, 1889, the law requiring electrical executions goes into effect, but until yesterday the amount and character of current required to make death certain and instantaneous had not been determined. The experiments upon dogs made last summer by Harold P. Brown, the electrical engineer, were criticized because the weight of the animals killed was less than that of a man, and it was supposed that more current would be required to kill a human being on that account. Yesterday afternoon Mr. Brown was given an opportunity to make a demonstration before Elbridge T. Gerry, author of the electrical execution law, and the committee appointed by the Medico-Legal Society to report on the best means of putting the law into effect. The experiments were made at Mr. Edison's laboratory at Orange, and the first victim was a calf weighing 124½ pounds. The calf was cut on the forward and on the spine behind the forehead, and sponge-covered plates, moistened in a solution of sulphate of zinc, were fastened in place. The resistance of the animal was 3,200 ohms. An alternating current of 700 volts was applied for 30 seconds and the animal was killed instantly. It was at once dissected by Drs. Ingram and Bleyer, but the brain, heart, and lungs were found to be in normal condition, and the meat was pronounced fit for food. One metal plate carrying the current touched the hair of the forehead and slightly burned it, but otherwise there were no external indications of injury.

The second calf weighed 145 pounds, and had a resistance of 1,300 ohms. The deadly alternating current at 700 volts pressure was applied for five seconds and produced instant death. To settle permanently the weight question, a horse weighing 1,230 pounds was next killed by passing the alternating current at 700 volts from one fore leg to the other. The resistance of this animal was 11,000 ohms. Mr. Brown was assisted by Dr. A. E. Kennelly, and there were present Thomas A. Edison, Prof. R. Ogden Doremus, Prof. Charles A. Doremus, Dr. Frederick Peterson, Dr. Frank H. Ingram, Elbridge T. Gerry, Mr. Galvin, Dr. J. M. Bloyer, Mr. Bourgouon, and John Murray Mitchell.

The experiments proved the alternating current to be the most deadly force known to science, and that less than half the pressure used in this city for electric lighting by this system is sufficient to cause instant death. After Jan. 1 the alternating current will undoubtedly drive the hangmen out of business in this State.

New York American, **February 10, 1905**

EDISON REGRETS ELECTRIC CHAIR WAS EVER INVENTED

BY JAMES S. EVANS

Not long ago Thomas A. Edison, the greatest living genius, was asked if he had invented the apparatus used in the two States where murderers are electrocuted—New York and Ohio. The question was put to him while he was in a state of great mental perturbation, but his face softened and his voice quickly lost its flinty substance when he replied to the question on electrocution.

"I did not invent such an instrument," he said, "and I am sorry that electricity has been put to such bad use. When the apparatus was being installed at Sing Sing I went up to look at it. The law providing for such means of death had passed—passed to the horror of all men with keen sensibilities, the love of humanity and the fear of God in their hearts. I may have contributed something toward simplifying the method of putting men to death, but if I did so I was moved by a spirit that meant less suffering for those condemned."

"Is electrocution the most painless way of putting one to death?"

"Assuredly it is. There is a sensation of a moment only—as quick as the bat of an eye. But in that second there is pain indescribable. The flash comes and the shock; it is ten times more excruciating than the feeling that results from one's placing his hands on live coals. It is a burning, devilish, harrowing feeling. Imagine the quick thrusting of ten thousand hot needle points into the body at one time, and you may have a faint idea of the shock when the current is turned on." His blue eyes fell on the crackling logs that lay burning in the big fireplace before him. For a minute he sat wrapped in gloomy meditation. Around him were miniature models of his greatest discoveries—the telephone, the graphophone [*sic*], the electric light, the phonograph, the storage battery—dozens of mechanical contrivances that have given the world incalculable benefits. His big yard dog that had been lying before the fire got up, yawned, stretched himself and then walked over and put his nose between his master's knees. The greatest electrical inventor the world has ever known thus was awakened from his reverie. He continued: "I am sorry the gallows was ever thought of; the guillotine is a barbarous instrument. The system of garroting belongs to the Dark Ages, and whatever may be said in behalf of the present way New York has of treating its murderers, it is no less ghastly and inexcusable than are the instruments of death used in the semi-civilized nations. . . .

X-Rays: Original Correspondence and News Items

1896–1897, 1904

After German scientist William Roentgen announced his discovery of x–rays in November 1895, Edison joined the rush to adapt this scientific discovery to practical uses. The leap toward experiments with human subjects was an obvious one. Doctors and patients as well as experimenters seized upon Roentgen's cathode tube for the purpose of medical imaging. The idea of a wholly new kind of ray captured Edison's attention, and he thought that commercial uses for x-rays would be pretty easy to develop. In typical Edison style, the inventor announced a discovery of his own within a few months: a better material basis for viewing the new images on fluorescent screens. Consequently, his mailbox was flooded with urgent requests from those who were hopeful that Edison's work with x-rays would improve the lot of suffering individuals and enhance the ability of doctors to treat their patients. Meanwhile, Edison and his employees unwittingly exposed themselves to potentially harmful doses of radiation. Fearlessly naïve, they soon learned the dangers of radiation.

Telegram from Edison to A. E. Kennelly, January 27, 1896

BETZ BUILDING
PHILADELPHIA, PENN.

How would you like to come over and experiment on Roentgen's new radiations? I have glassblower and pumps running and all photographic apparatus. We could do a lot before others get their second wind.

Edison

Jerome Carty to Edison, February 12, 1896

PHILADELPHIA

My Dear Mister Edison:
You probably remember me by reason of our interviews in regard to the Edison-Kenny Autographic patent.
    I now take the liberty of writing you upon a subject of great anxiety and sorrow to me, and which may interest you, at least I hope it will.

In October 1894 my wife met with a very serious and almost fatal accident in a folding bed of the Standard make, which fell over upon us, and caught her in the act of lying down. She was doubled or so twisted as to remain unconscious for some hours, and was delirious for several weeks. During the first six weeks her life was despaired of, but gradually she has recovered her general health, both mentally and physically, but she is paralyzed from the abdomen down to the feet, and unable to move. We have had prominent physicians, and she has had the best of care, but to no avail. An operation has been suggested, but it is said to be dangerous. Would your experiments in the Cathode Rays avail to assist you in locating the seat of her injury, if so, she is at your service, and I know if you could spare an hour from your busy surrounding to see her it would do her a world of good. We are located at No. 96 N. 18th Street, East Orange [New Jersey], where the accident happened. I will be glad to call and explain more fully if you desire.

I am generally at home Saturday afternoons and Sundays. If you cannot call perhaps you may suggest some one to see her. Ordinary medical help seemed to have failed.

>Yours very truly,
>Jerome Carty [Attorney, Patent and Trade Mark Cases]

Edison to Carty [draft reply scrawled on Carty's letter]

Two [*sic*] early to make practical experiments. It requires every moment of my time to increase power of apparatus.

W. B. Hill to Edison, February 17, 1896

>40 CARROL ST., LOWER YONKERS, N.Y.

Dear Sir:

Being a perfect stranger I should not take the liberty of addressing you if not in the interest of humanity and science. In the school where I teach there are between four & five hundred pupils, all "deaf & dumb" so called. This is only a small fraction of the number similarly afflicted in this country. I have often thought that science would sooner or later come to their relief. It may be too much to hope, but do you not think that these newly discovered X rays might be of great assistance. If we could only get a picture of the bones in the ear, it might go a long way to solving the problem. I would make some experiments myself if I only had the means.

You have done so much to lift the burdens of the world, that I naturally turned to you as most likely to be successful.

Yours in scientific fellowship,
W. B. Hill

Edison to W. B. Hill [draft reply scrawled on Hill's letter]

I intend trying to photo the inner ear soon and will let you know if I succeed.

New York World, **August 15, 1897**

THE X-RAY IS A SKIN BEAUTIFIER

EDISON AND ELIHU THOMPSON PROVE THAT IT SOFTENS AND CLEARS THE CUTICLE

BETTER THAN ANY COSMETIC AND LASTING IN EFFECT

The X rays have been found to have an entirely new and unexpected utility. . . . The X-ray burn, as it has been called, resembles the ordinary burn or scald, and has been supposed to be more or less dangerous. It is this so-called burning which, if allowed to act for sufficient length of time, works such wonders in refining and clearing the skin.

For some time Edison has been conducting experiments with the X-rays in his laboratory. . . . The work has been carried on by four men under his superintendence. A few weeks ago Mr. Edison decided that it would not be safe to subject himself to the action of the rays. He found that the skin of his hand was being slowly burned away. One of the men in the laboratory suffered even more from these curious burns, his skin becoming wrinkled and charred. After he had kept away from the X-rays it was found that these burns healed very rapidly. The skin which had been so discolored . . . grew again very much softer and whiter than before.

To produce this effect has been the object of all the makers of cosmetics for centuries. Edison pronounces the X-rays a positive beautifier. The most exact scientific knowledge on the subject is that collected by Elihu Thompson. Several theories have been advanced to account for the X-ray burns. One of these is that the mischief is caused by the ozone which is always to be found near the tubes. It is claimed by some that the electricity has a disintegrating effect. In order to set at rest these doubtful theories Prof. Thompson carried

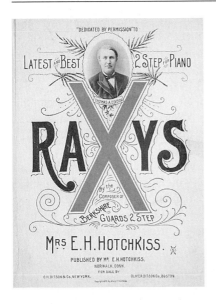

X-Ray Sheet Music A sheet music cover for a topical two-step from 1896 celebrates Edison's work with x-rays. No one yet knew how dangerous x-rays could be.
Courtesy of the Edison National Historic Site, National Park Service, U.S. Department of the Interior.

out an exhaustive series of experiments . . . cheerfully giving himself up as a sacrifice to the cause. . . .

It will, of course, have to be found by experience just how these rays should be applied in order to produce the rejuvenating effects desired. . . . The X-ray burn really serves to remove the outer covering of the skin, and allow a new, and therefore whiter, and purer skin to grow in its place. The X-ray may be compared to an exaggerated case of sunburn. It is in reality a cross between a regular scald and a scorch. . . .

Schenectady Union, October 5, 1904

MARTYR TO SCIENCE

CANCER RESULT OF LONG EXPERIMENTING WITH X-RAYS

After seven years of incessant suffering, Clarence M. Dally, who was affected by the X-ray when experimenting under the direction of Thomas A. Edison, is dead at his home in East Orange. Seven operations were performed from time to time in attempts to stop the disease that had attacked him, but eventually his entire system was affected and he sank slowly to death. Dally's case has been followed with interest by medical men in all parts of this country and Europe. . . . his wonderful battle against the creeping disease resulted in material addition to the scientific knowledge of X-ray burns. . . .

At the experimental work with the X-ray . . . Dally was Edison's chief assistant. He was so engrossed in his work he spent only a few hours a day away from the laboratory. . . . his hands were repeatedly being brought into the flood of the X-rays. Mr. Edison himself was burned slightly in these experiments and his recovery was slow.

Red Patches, But No Pain.   Dally, however, was brought within range of the light more frequently than his chief, and nothing that science could do for him wrought any permanent good. Small round red patches appeared on his hands. They looked like scalds . . . no pain accompanied them. The spots appeared seven years ago, and at first Dally paid little attention to them.

In four months the hands began to swell. Two months later Dally was forced to abandon all work in the laboratory, and spent his time setting X-ray instruments in order in hospitals and colleges. He kept at that work for two years, his hands meanwhile becoming more and more affected. Soon his hands began to pain. So intense was his suffering that he found it necessary to sleep at night in a narrow cot, with a hand over each side, resting in a shallow receptacle filled with water. . . .

Skin Grafting Failed.   Just when it seemed the trouble had been checked cancer attacked his left wrist. . . . In February 1902 more than 150 pieces of skin were taken from his legs and grafted on his hands. But . . . the operation was not a success.

After that the disease developed rapidly, and on August 16, 1902 his left arm was amputated four inches from the shoulder. For three months it seemed Dally was improving, but on November 20, 1902, the little finger on his right hand became affected, and it was taken off. Dally still thought he would recover. He did not lose heart when, on June 16, 1903, the other fingers on that hand were cut off. . . .

Loses His Other Arm.   In March of this year the disease had reached such a stage that the doctors decided on amputation, and on March 16 the right forearm was cut off four inches below the elbow. The wound quickly healed and Dally's spirits rose. He clung to life desperately, and so sure was he that he at last had lost all traces of the disease that he had artificial arms made. He wore them just a week; then the disease attacked his entire system. That was early in the summer, and since then he had been failing gradually.

Storage Batteries: Press Notices and a Letter

1899, 1902, 1912

By the mid-1890s, Edison was working intensively to make electric storage batteries of his own design that could serve as an effective power source for propelling electric vehicles and trolleys.[2] *From his very first days as a telegrapher, Edison had worked with batteries, and he knew their shortcomings. The usual wet cell batteries needed frequent attention to remain even modestly efficient, and they suffered leaks and spills, exposing their handlers to noxious chemicals. Beginning around 1899, Edison turned his attention to the problems he had so long contemplated. In 1901 he started the Edison Storage Battery Company to develop, manufacture, and sell rechargeable (i.e., storage) batteries. For much of the following decade he would try to bring out a storage battery that met his criteria: efficient, durable, and lighter than the lead-containing storage batteries that other companies sold. He was not about to produce an electric horse, but rather sought to provide the means to make better electric vehicles, and to explain why electric vehicles were advantageous. Decades of testing and modifications followed, as he worked out all of the kinks, or "bugs," as even Edison liked to call imperfections in technology.*

New York Dry Good Economist, September 16, 1899

EDISON AND THE AUTOMOBILE

. . . A CHEAP AUTOMOBILE NEEDED

Quick as ever to grasp a situation, the inventor has evidently foreseen the need of [an automobile that will be within the reach of the average person]—one that will cost less than two hundred and fifty dollars, and consequently be within the means of the horse-owner of today. If the horse is to be superseded by the motor car, it must be by means of

---

[2]At the beginning of the twentieth century, Edison owned all three representative types of motorized cars currently available for personal mobility: a steam car, an electrically powered vehicle, and a gasoline-fueled car with an internal combustion engine.

a vehicle that costs less than the animal. If it costs more it will not be generally used. The cumbrous electric cab now used, heavy and inartistic as it is, costs two thousand dollars, but it is Mr. Edison's purpose to reduce the price to five hundred dollars, to make it lighter and more pleasing to the eye. Once he can demonstrate that a cab can be produced on the above lines, he will extend the principle to hundreds of other styles and sizes of vehicles, some of which will be put on the market, in all probability, as low as one hundred and fifty dollars apiece.

The Approach of the Horseless Age.   Something of the magnitude of the field in which Mr. Edison's efforts are now being directed may be gathered from the figures of recent incorporations. Six companies are now organized, and three of them are engaged in the manufacture of horseless vehicles. The aggregate capital of the six companies is eighty million. Several kinds are made in the United States, including gasoline vehicles and storage battery electric cabs. The average cost of the former is twelve hundred dollars, and of the latter two thousand dollars. The gasoline motor costs less to run, as it does not require over a gallon of the fluid to make a trip of fifteen miles; whereas, an electric wagon must be recharged every trip of fifteen miles at considerably more expense. The automobile is rapidly assuming a definite place in the public mind, and this condition is bound to result in an extended market as soon as construction can be simplified and the price reduced. The United States government has taken the first steps looking to the use of electric mail wagons for both collection and delivery purposes. . . .

North American Review, July 1902

"THE STORAGE BATTERY AND THE MOTOR CAR"

BY THOMAS A. EDISON

The final perfection of the storage battery, which I believe has been accomplished, will in my opinion bring about a multitude of changes and improvements in our business and social economy. No one of these will interest the public more just now than the doing away with the chauffeur, the irresponsible instrument, in the public eye at least, of so many recent accidents with automobiles.

Of the new storage battery, which was admirably described in *Harper's Weekly* last December, and about which a great many erroneous and unauthorized statements have since been made, I can now say that it has sustained and overcome the four thorough tests applied to it, and it is now, at this writing, undergoing the fifth, and last, with every prospect of the same result. . . .

In spite of assertions to the contrary, I think the storage battery carriage, by the aid of the new battery, will come ultimately within the reach of the man of moderate means. Driving through the many miles of streets in the suburbs of New York, I have been impressed with the fact that something like eighty per cent of the residences have no carriage houses. The storage battery carriage, with the new battery, should enable the owners of forty percent of these residences to have a serviceable pleasure vehicle at their beck and call, without hiring a coachman to keep it clean and run it, with no horses to eat their heads off and no oats and hay to buy. With an initial outlay of from $700 and upwards, the storage battery automobile can be used once a week at the cost of a fifty-cent charge, or twice for a dollar, and so on, the cost of use being met as it is incurred and so ceasing to be the bugbear that fixed charges must always be to the householder of moderate income. . . .

. . . The electric carriage of the future, and of the near future, will in my opinion not only supersede other types of automobiles, but will be built and run on such practical lines that accidents will soon become things of the past. Horse owners and drivers will educate their animals, as in old times they had to be educated up to the steam engine and later to the trolley car. The electric carriage will be practically noiseless and easily stopped in an emergency. Above all, it will need no irresponsible chauffeur. . . .

Edison to Irving Bloomingdale, April 16, 1912

59TH ST. & 3RD AVE., NEW YORK CITY

Dear Sir:
On my return from Florida, where I have been for a month, I find a letter from Mr. Arthur Williams of the New York Edison Co., in which he states that he has had a conversation with you in regard to delivery wagons [for your department store]. I have written to Mr. Williams in reply, stating that I would also write to you direct.

Over a year ago I became convinced that there could be constructed a light electric delivery wagon to take the place of the one horse wagon, and that it could be operated with greater economy than the horse wagon. I commenced a series of experiments in the construction of such a vehicle and sent my assistant to visit various large concerns in order to obtain reliable data as to the cost of delivery with horse wagons. Among those visited was your own firm and you very kindly contributed to the data which he was gathering for me, and which has been of considerable value and has been reserved exclusively for my own personal use.

Ever since the early part of the summer we have been running our experimental vehicles over the hardest kind of roads in order to [reveal] weaknesses of construction. In so doing we have constantly brought out defects, all of which have been eliminated from time to time so that our vehicle as at present developed looks as if it would stand almost anything. I am now experimenting to reduce the friction in order to economize in current consumed in running the wagon. As soon as I have the wagon in shape satisfactory to me, I shall let you know, and would very much like to have you or one of your representatives come over and see it.

It may also interest you to learn that for the past six months we have been running a hard road test to destroy a one ton delivery wagon made by an outside manufacturer for one of the Express Companies. This you could also see and examine the data.

Yours very truly,
[Thomas A. Edison]

Concrete Houses: News Items and Original Correspondence
1901, 1907–1909

In 1899 Edison started the Edison Portland Cement Company to manufacture and sell cement. He built a mill in western New Jersey, near his quarry, and he experimented with grinding and crushing technology as well as with the kilns required to prepare cement. As with his storage batteries, Edison's new endeavor involved the creation of new markets for the product he was trying to sell. The most inventive of Edison's schemes to stimulate demand for cement was his idea for pouring concrete into a giant mold to result in a whole house. He envisioned vast suburbs of poured concrete houses: Construction companies would achieve economies of scale by building many homes at once, so consumers would be able to buy them for a fraction of what they might otherwise cost. Predictably, Edison announced his intentions before he could actually pour houses.

Just as predictably, his idea was carried in newspapers around the world and became the subject of great acclaim. Like Henry Ford's 1914 announcement that he would increase the pay of working men to five dollars a day, Edison's affordable house was an ambitious response to ongoing concerns about the ill effects of rapid industrialization and urbanization. Despite some serious interest in Edison's ideas, only a few homes were ever built using his methods, and the inventor himself had no interest in constructing them himself.

Insurance Engineering, Interview with Edison, June 1901

Q. Is it your opinion that cement is to be the building material of the future?

A. Yes, that and steel. That is to say, cement combined with steel.

Q. Will you cite some examples of the present building materials which, in your opinion will be displaced by cement?

A. My impression is that the time will come when every contractor will have standard forms of houses, 20 or 30 varieties. The forms will be made of wood, and a contractor using one of the standard shapes will simply go out and "pour" a house. There will probably be hundreds of designs. The contractors will put up their concrete mixer, and have their beams and forms ready. They will pour the form for the first story; complete that; then pour the second story, and so on. To do that all they will require will be common labor—a few men, and one boss. That is what I think will be done eventually. And such a house can be made very cheaply. It means to me there will not be much use for carpenters then. There will be cabinet makers, to be sure. Why even the floors and stairs will be made of concrete.

Q. Will Portland cement be cheap enough for general use?

A. Yes, I think so. When the price gets to be one dollar a barrel or five dollars a ton, and people know they can get it for that, there will be enormous quantities of it used. . . .

Q. Have you seen any account of the church in Brooklyn, on the corner of Lafayette Avenue and St. James Place, built up section by section precisely as you have described?

A. No; but that is the way to do it. Houses built in that manner can be rented profitably for, say, seven or eight dollars a month. They will be cheap as that. And a house can be put up and completed in a few days. The architects will have a fine time, for they can pour statuary and all sorts of ornamentation while they are completing the walls. . . . If the contractors have the proper molds, there will not be any difficulty in making the most beautiful houses wonderfully cheap.

Q. Will the use of cement modify the construction of high buildings?

A. All those buildings will be of steel construction with Portland cement . . .

New York Herald, **November 9, 1907**

CITY OF CONCRETE

Working together, Thomas A. Edison . . . and Henry Phipps, a New York millionaire, believe they can solve the problem of tenement housing. Mr. Edison having perfected plans recently whereby, he says, he can build within twelve hours and at a cost of from $1,000 to $1,200 a beautiful nine-room house, suitable for two families. Each apartment of these double houses can be rented profitably at $7.50 a month, according to Mr. Edison, thus saving to the working man now paying $10 a month for a two room home in the tenements, enough money to cover his carfare expenses to and from work. . . . Mr. Phipps, who in 1905 gave $1,000,000 for the erection of model tenements in New York City, spent yesterday afternoon in Mr. Edison's laboratory . . . discussing with him the possibilities of the cement or concrete house. The steel manufacturer was accompanied by a corps of architects, builders and concrete experts who made a careful investigation of the Edison plans. When they left they were enthusiastic over its possibilities. Mr. Edison proposes to build these houses by forcing a concrete mixture into cast iron molds, which are to be set up after the excavation is complete.

He has a model of such a house now . . . and he is working on plans for the mold in which the full sized double residences will be created. . . . If it proves satisfactory Mr. Phipps and other wealthy men expect to take hold of the project and erect a large number of these houses near New York City. The white haired inventor was poring over a mass of figures in his laboratory yesterday afternoon, when a reporter from the *Herald* saw him. He spoke in short, quick sentences and in five minutes said more than the average man says in thirty.

"Yes, Mr. Phipps and his experts have been here all afternoon investigating my cement house," said Mr. Edison. "He is seeking as I am, to help the man who works in the ditch and who can only afford a

Edison and Concrete House Model Edison's concrete houses were designed to be poured all at once, using giant metal molds. Several were eventually built and proved very successful as dwellings, but Edison's dreams of whole poured suburban neighborhoods were never realized.
Courtesy of the Edison National Historic Site, National Park Service, U.S. Department of the Interior.

two room apartment in some slum tenement for himself and his family." "Mr. Phipps thinks as I do, that my house will solve this problem. It is for me to build one of these houses, to create the unity. Some one else must build the city, and Mr. Phipps seems to be the proper man to put it up."

Henry Phipps to Edison, November 13, 1907

787 FIFTH AVENUE, NEW YORK

My Dear Mr. Edison:
Many thanks for your kind attentions yesterday to my friends and myself. We enjoyed very much seeing you, and learning more of the good work you have in hand in respect to concrete construction.

If it is proper for us to make a suggestion we would beg to say that we wish the liberal experiment you are about to make were done on a smaller scale, and a simpler house, so as to save you money, and a good deal of care and trouble as well, and to aid the good cause which you especially, and the rest of us, have at heart.

Please pardon the suggestion we have made, and believe me,

Yours sincerely,
Henry Phipps

Edison to Henry Phipps, November 15, 1907

My Dear Mr. Phipps—
I think it would be an error not to build the most beautiful house that is possible, the extra cost of the molds as against a plain box is not so great as one would imagine. If the slums of the cities can be depopulated by building rows of plain boxes & in no other way then that is the way to do it, but if the same result can be attained and by making these houses as beautiful as art can make them, then I think it would be a sad mistake not to do so.

Henry Phipps to Edison, November 22, 1907

Dear Mr. Edison:
I thank you for your kind note.

The question before us is—what can we do in the way of furnishing a cheap house for "The man in the ditch"? I think with you that concrete is the material. What will put it together most cheaply is the question—no doubt steel moulds. In the beginning I think we should aim at simplicity; that is make a house for the very poor man we desire to benefit. Mr. Atterbury has a plan for making house room by room, which is surely fast enough, and would avoid an enormous outlay at the beginning. What we need is a warm dry house before we consider the aesthetic side. In the evolution of man adornment comes last. Nature begins with small things and works up to man, and so in building these homes, let us begin on the simplest and cheapest plan. . . . Later on we can build for the better wage earner. . . ."[3]

Grand Rapids (Michigan) *Evening Press*, July 9, 1909

EDISON'S POURED CEMENT HOUSE HERE

A home builder whose work will affect vitally the inner life of the next generation, this is Thomas A. Edison, come to fulfill the promise of Emerson.

The wizard of East Orange will wave his wand and presto—A house complete, upstairs, downstairs, basement, attic, finished even to decorated landings, postals, closets, bathtubs, chandeliers—all ready for Mr. Groom and his bride to step into. . . .

The poured cement house—after eight years of experimenting and two years of uninterrupted hard work, is ready. He will pour his first building in East Orange in August.

When wizard Edison's plan became public two years ago a howl of disbelief and ridicule went up. "Impracticable," the contractors said.

"A village of houses all exactly alike—what nonsense," exclaimed the architects.

BUT EDISON MADE GOOD.

. . . Here is a thumbnail description of a house as it will come from the mold:

Size—Twenty-five by thirty feet ground plan.

Rooms—Big living room and kitchen on first floor, two big bedrooms, wide hallway, closets and bath upstairs, front and back porch.

Cost—About $1,200

---

[3] Edison preferred his own ideas; collaboration with Phipps did not progress. Examples of Edison's concrete houses were eventually built in northern New Jersey, but large-scale housing developments were never attempted. Though the houses came in several slightly different styles, consumers apparently resisted their sameness. Vast suburban developments of "cookie-cutter" houses (like Levittown, N.Y.) would not be built until after World War II.

Material—Light gray re-enforced concrete

Time to Mold—Fourteen days.

Decorations—Facades and ornamental work along the porch, carved stone pillars in hallways, window seats and paneled doors with mythological figuring, gabled roofs.

Special advantages—Fireproof and vermin proof; no repairs

The people it will benefit particularly—The workingmen who now often live in uncomfortable dwellings.

Inventor—Thomas A. Edison.

The Edison house, if it accomplishes half what its creator expects, will revolutionize house building.

One big important thing he had in mind was to make it possible for people of the slums to live in houses that would be clean, have plenty of light and air, and which could be had at a moderate cost.

The inventor will not build houses himself. He has more important work to do. He has shown the world the way to do it, and will leave it at that.

Objections Overcome. Several great objections which arose two years ago had to be overcome by Edison in his later plans.

One—a practical builder's objection—was that the cement could not be forced through an intricate set of molds and be of the same consistency and strength throughout. Also that the surface would not be smooth.

But Edison produced a cement of a consistency almost like water, which holds the stone and aggregates equally throughout. It will also secure a surface so smooth that it can be painted or frescoed or tinted.

Another objection was that it would be impossible to build the molds which would make inner rooms and closets. This too has been overcome.

Still another—this time from architects—was that all the houses would be alike, necessarily; that people would not live in them on that account. But the Edison moulds are adapted to a number of variations. With six sets . . . which the inventor reckons as the right number for a good working arrangement, an immensely wide variety of houses may be constructed. . . .

Motion Pictures

The long excerpt from the earliest history of motion pictures and the short program for distribution at film exhibitions that follow together offer a rare glimpse at the very beginning of motion pictures in the United States. When the Dicksons wrote their History of the Kineto-graph *nothing about the future of these new mechanical amusements seemed certain, except their capacity to provoke wonder. W. K. L. Dickson and his boss, Edison, were still engaged with nonprojected motion pictures, and still hoping to synchronize moving pictures with sound. Audiences watched tiny animated figures by individually looking down into a "peep-hole" kinetoscope. The Dicksons' history vouches for Edison's early work in the field while it also describes the subject matter of the earliest films that emerged from the laboratory practices of Edison's West Orange complex. By the time the next document, the program, was prepared, films were projected onto screens. Short films with a variety of subjects were shown one after another and often as part of a longer program of nonfilm entertainment. This program hints at some of the ongoing construction of motion pictures as both realistic or "lifelike" and (at least potentially) tasteful or "high-class." Documents that reflect the later development of motion pictures as modern mass media appear below in the following sections.*

From *History of the Kinetograph, Kinetoscope, and Kineto-phonograph,* 1895

BY W. K. L. DICKSON AND ANTONIA DICKSON

In the year 1887, Mr. Edison found himself in possession of one of those breathing spells which relieve the tension of inventive thought. The great issues of electricity were satisfactorily under way. The incandescent light had received its finishing touches; telephonic and telegraphic devices were substantially interwoven with the fabric of international life; the phonograph was established upon what seemed to be a solid financial and social basis, and the inventor felt at liberty to indulge in a few secondary flights of fancy. It was then that he was struck by the idea of reproducing to the eye the effect of motion by means of a swift and graded succession of pictures and of linking these photographic impressions with the phonograph in one combination so as to complete to both senses synchronously the record of a given scene. At the time of which we speak the conditions of photography were eminently favorable as a basis for experiments, while their obvious limitations afforded a tempting field for further research. The initial crudities of Daguerre, Niepce, and their peers had been successfully tested and superseded, and the science was now enriched by the discoveries of Maddox, author of the bromo-gelatine process of instantaneous photography. The initial principle of moving images was suggested by a toy, familiar to children as the zoetrope, or wheel of life, a contrivance consisting of a cylinder some ten inches wide, open at the top, around the lower and interior rim of which a series of related pictures is placed, representing any given phase of life, susceptible of swift and continuous motion. The cylinder is then rapidly rotated, and the eye of the spectator, being directed to the narrow and vertical slits on the outer surface of the cylinder, is edified by a series of painfully spasmodic jerks which by the exercise of a liberal fancy may pass as dimly suggestive of human and equine antics. This effect, as the reader probably knows, springs from the substitution of one succeeding phase of an attitude for another so as to produce the effect of continuity upon the retina, and the failure of these successive images to blend into an illusive picture is due to the roughness of the woodcuts and the impossibility of obtaining the requisite degree of speed. The idea, however, was a novel and ingenious one, and as such commended itself to the attention of photographic experts such as Mr. Muybridge and others, who, working upon the delicately responsive surface of the Maddox dry gelatin plate, were able to secure greatly superior results. Despite the important improvements, however, the system presented grave imperfections, and the limited speed attainable militated hopelessly against the desired realism of effect. It was then that a series of experiments was entered upon at the Orange Laboratory, extending over a period of six years.

The synchronous attachment of photography with the phonograph was early contemplated in order to record and give back the impressions to the eye as well as to the ear. The comprehensive term for this invention is the kineto-phonograph. The dual taking machine is the phono-kinetograph, and the reproducing machine is the phono-kineto-scope, in contradistinction to the kinetograph and kinetoscope, which apply respectively to the taking and reproduction of movable but *soundless* objects.

The initial experiments took the form of microscopic pinpoint photographs, placed on a cylindrical shell, corresponding in size to the ordinary phonograph cylinder. These two cylinders were then placed

Edison Kinetoscope Unlike the first motion pictures in Europe, Edison's motion pictures were not projected. Instead, viewers looked down into a cabinet (opened at the back in this historic photograph), where they watched a long loop of film offer the impression of tiny moving subjects.
Courtesy of the Edison National Historic Site, National Park Service, U.S. Department of the Interior.

side by side on a shaft, and the sound record was taken as near as possible synchronously with the photographic image, impressed on the sensitive surface of the shell. The photographic portion of the undertaking was seriously hampered by the materials at hand, which, however excellent in themselves, offered no substance sufficiently sensitive. How to secure clear-cut outlines, or indeed any outlines at all, together with phenomenal speed, was the problem which puzzled the experimenters. . . .

The next step was the adoption of a highly sensitized strip of celluloid, one half inch wide, but this proving unsatisfactory, owing to inadequate size, one inch pictures were substituted on a band one and a half inches wide, the additional width being required for the perforations on the outer edge. . . .

The establishment of harmonious relations between kinetograph and phonograph was a harrowing task and would have broken the spirit of inventors less inured to hardship and discouragement than Edison's veterans. . . . The experiments have borne their legitimate fruit, and the most scrupulous nicety of adjustment has been achieved, with the resultant effects of realistic life, audibly and visually expressed. . . . The crowning point of realism was attained on the occasion of Mr. Edison's return from the Paris Exposition of 1889, when Mr. Dickson himself stepped out on the screen, raised his hat and smiled, while uttering the words of greeting, "Good morning, Mr. Edison, glad to see you back. I hope you are satisfied with the kineto-phonograph."[4]

The photographic rooms, with their singular completeness of appointment, have been the birth-place and nursery of the kinetoscope; and the other important processes connected with the preparation and development of the film, together with innumerable other mechanical and scientific devices, are still carried on in this department. The exigencies of natural lighting, however, incident to the better "taking" of the subjects and the lack of a suitable theatrical stage, necessitated the construction of a special building, which stands in the center of that cluster of auxiliary houses which forms the suburbs of the laboratory. . . .

[On the first film subjects:]

No department of the wizard's domains is more fraught with perennial interest than this theater; none are more interwoven with the laughter, the pathos, the genius and the dexterities of life. . . . The *Dramatis Personae* of this stage are recruited from every characteristic section of social, artistic and industrial life, and from every conceivable phase of animal existence within the scope of laboratory enterprise. Bucking broncos, terriers and rats, accomplished dogs who turn somersaults and describe serpentine dances, trained lions,

---

[4]Efforts to synchronize motion pictures and phonographs continued off and on for decades. Edison demonstrated his "kinetophone" publicly in 1910, but it was never commercially successful.

bears and monkeys are among the stars of this unique company. On one occasion, the platform was occupied by a wire cage, the sometime arena for certain gallinaceous conflicts [i.e., cockfights]. A duel between two aspiring and vindictive roosters took place and the films have registered the strut, the swagger and the general bravado of the feathered knights. Another day chronicled the engagement of a troupe of trained bears and their leaders, Hungarians by nationality, to whom the scientific eccentricities of the laboratory furnish an inexhaustible mine of wealth. The theatre at such times might move "the inextinguishable laughter of the blessed gods," and peals of these tantalizing cachinnations are borne to the envious ears of dwellers in distant settlements, grim genii of the dynamo and ore milling departments [of the lab]. . . .

Organ grinders and monkeys have contributed liberally to the kinetographic collection. It is estimated that the classic soil of New Jersey supports three of these itinerant musicians to each square mile, while denying its patronage to [highbrow professionals like] Seidel or Damrosch. It may, therefore, be inferred that artistic supplies, of this nature at least, are in no immediate danger of depletion. Every few days a native of sunny Italy may be seen describing his eccentric orbit in the direction of the Orange Laboratory, intoning his torturous strains and administering finishing touches to the decayed elegance of the monkey's attire. No perceptible chasm differentiates employer and employee. Both are draped in picturesque remnants, both reside on the frayed outskirts of society, both are the victims of insatiable curiosity. On one occasion the nickel and slot was on view, a machine which, claiming only to be a duodecimo edition of the kinetoscope, and designed to meet the popular requirements on a simple and inexpensive basis, is limited in its scope, and admits only of a single spectator at a time, which is supposed to glue his eyes to the narrow opening at the top. It so happens that master and monkey were simultaneously stricken with the desire to see, an impulse which brought their heads into sharp contact and led to much energetic cuffing and chattering. The poor little ape went to the wall, as is generally the case with poor relations, and the Italian regaled himself with a long contemplation of his charms, after which he vacated in favor of his slave, whose delight was unbounded at the spectacle of these diminutive doubles, performing the familiar round of the itinerant repertoire. It is on record that the tiny creature laughed, actually laughed, oblivious for a few enchanted seconds of unkind man, of sunless cellars, starvation and chastisement, and the tribute is accepted as one of the most gratifying in all the archives of the sated kinetoscope. . . .

Of human subjects we have a superfluity, although the utmost discrimination has been observed in the selection of themes. In point of classical beauty and as a prophetic exposition of what we may expect in the physical regeneration of the race, Eugen Sandow, the modern Hercules, stands foremost. . . . That his agility is equal to his strength is shown in the exploit known as the Roman column, where, with knees chained to an iron column, he bends backwards to the ground, lifting huge dumb-bells and three men to show the use of the dorsal and abdominal muscles. Many of his feats and poses are modeled upon the pictured achievements of ancient bards and sculptors, and the effect is artistically perfect.

In the suggestion of unguessed planes of virility, Buffalo Bill and his motley suite have materially assisted. Nothing more stimulating can be imagined than these unconventional types of humanity, these riotous Texan cow-boys and Mexicans, these Moors, Arabs and Indians, riding, lassoing, shooting, juggling and sparring with the swiftness and ease born of untrammeled physical conditions. Unique in interest also is the Omaha war dance, the Sioux ghost dance and Indian war council, features of aboriginal life which may be historically valuable long after our polished continent has parted with the last races of her romantic past. . . .

The advantages to students and historians will be immeasurable. Instead of dry and misleading accounts, tinged with the exaggerations of the chroniclers' minds, our archives will be enriched by the vitalized pictures of great national scenes, instinct with all the glowing personalities which characterized them.

What is the future of the kinetograph? Ask rather, from what conceivable phase of the future it can be debarred. In the promotion of business interests, in the advancement of science, in the revelation of unguessed worlds, in its educational and re-creative powers, and in its ability to immortalize our fleeting but beloved associations, the kinetograph stands foremost among the creations of modern inventive genius. It is the crown and flower of nineteenth-century magic. . . .

Program for Projected Films (n.d.)

The World's Greatest Sensation
Edison's Startling Invention
Those Immense Life Motion Pictures

Many New Subjects
Read This.

This entertainment is nothing like the old magic-lantern, steropticon or dissolving views we have seen, but Edison's great invention, showing immense pictures, actually alive, battleships, soldiers, cavalry and other scenes in full action. If your own family photographs were taken by this new process you would appear alive and full size on the canvas, not sitting still, as in ordinary photographs, but actually walking back and forth, full life size, laughing and shaking hands as if really alive. Thus every variety of living, moving scenes . . . both on land and sea, will be shown on the immense canvas in real life movements so natural you would feel that horses and men would actually leave the canvas and come dashing into the audience as they gallop by. The several exciting war scenes, express trains at full speed, fierce, dashing fire brigades, and many such scenes are so thrilling that persons in the audience often say they feel like moving from their seats to escape from harm. The pictures are life size, clear and bright, and steady in motion. The principle will be illustrated. No one who has not seen this masterpiece of the great Edison can afford to miss this opportunity.

Laing Bros.

High-Class Programs

Media and Politics

One of the most obvious ways in which phonograph records and motion pictures shaped modern experience was in their wide circulation of "hits" and news. Recording and photography attested to the "real" events of the day, supplementing newspapers, which continued to provide literate Americans with a daily ritual of consuming and belonging in the modern world. The promotional literature and news items presented in this section show the ways in which records and films first became engaged in American political life at the level of presidential inaugurations, elections, and assassinations. Motion pictures made at the time of President William McKinley's assassination, for example, foreshadow and can be no less carefully considered for their documentary qualities than the Zapruder film made at the time of President John F. Kennedy's assassination. Phonograph recordings of sound bites by candidates for President in 1908, although they likely had little success in stores (musical records were far more popular), prefigured the packaging of candidates and "sound bites" for later broadcast media.

FILMS ADVERTISED TO THE TRADE, 1901–1902

From the Catalog of July 1901

PRESIDENT MCKINLEY TAKING THE OATH OF OFFICE.

This picture opens by showing the Diplomatic Corps, accompanied by Admiral Dewey and General Nelson A. Miles, coming down the carpeted stone steps of the Capitol and going to their seats in front of the stand where the President speaks. Next come the members of the President's Cabinet, and they are followed closely by President McKinley, preceded by Sergeant-at-Arms Randsdell of the Senate, bare headed and one armed, and also accompanied by the joint committee of Congress. . . . The President then steps promptly to the front of the stand amid the cheers of the immense crowd who stand with heads reverently uncovered, filling the entire foreground of our picture. As the tumult ceases, Chief Justice Melville W. Fuller, in the black silk robes of his high office, steps forward and holding in his outstretched hand a small Bible, administers the oath of office. The oath taken, the President presses his lips to the Bible and with manuscript in hand immediately begins his speech.   Length 50 feet. $7.50

Note: Again the valuable and exclusive privileges granted us by the United States Government allowed us to place the camera within fifteen feet of the President when he took the oath of office. We regret that we were unable to secure a longer film than listed above, but the rain began falling in torrents with almost the first words of the President's speech, which of course prohibited our taking a greater length of film, but notwithstanding the fact that it began sprinkling before the President took the oath of office, the fifty feet of film which we did secure is good.

From the Catalog of September 1902

Our cameras were at work at the Pan-American Exposition during President McKinley's entire visit, and we recorded many scenes incidental to the coming and going of the Presidential party. We were also fortunate enough to have our camera in position while President

McKinley was making his speech at the Pan-American Exposition on Thursday, September 5th, 1901, and thus secured a picture of our Executive while making the last address before the cowardly assault upon his life. On Friday, September 6th, 1901, we also had our cameras in position to photograph the President as he left the Temple of Music, but the deplorable assassination, of course, prevented our getting this picture. We did, however, secure an excellent panoramic view of the mob surging in front of the temple of Music attempting to get at the assassin. These pictures have created intense excitement and interest. In addition to being the best and easiest recognized view of the President and Mrs. McKinley, they depict the last acts of our beloved ruler before he was shot. Our cameras were the only ones at work at the Pan-American Exposition on the day of President McKinley's speech, Thursday, September 5th, and on Friday, September 6th, the day of the shooting. We secured the only animate pictures incidental to these events.

PANORAMIC VIEW OF THE CROWD RUSHING FOR THE CITY HALL, BUFFALO, TO VIEW THE BODY OF PRESIDENT MCKINLEY

This picture shows immense crowds in the background held in check by soldiers and policemen. Immediately the President's body rests upon the catafalque in the rotunda of the City Hall, the ropes which held the crowd in check are removed and a great rush is made for the City Hall entrance. The profound respect and reverence in which the President is held is here demonstrated, as the police check the entire multitude by simply raising their hands to them, and they immediately form in an orderly procession four abreast and quietly await their turn to pass in and view their beloved ruler.   Class A   50 ft. $7.50

With the exception of the portion of the film where the President's body was carried into the City Hall, a pouring rain was falling during the exposure of the pictures. While the President's body was being transferred from the hearse to City Hall a singular occurrence took place. The rain ceased falling almost simultaneous with the body being lifted from the hearse and the sun burst forth during the brief interval that was necessary to carry the casket to its resting place. Immediately the body had passed into the City Hall the sky became clouded and rain began falling again. . . .

THE MARTYRED PRESIDENTS—LINCOLN, GARFIELD, MCKINLEY

We have just finished and now offer to exhibitors a picture which we consider most valuable as an ending to the series of McKinley funeral pictures. The scene opens with a beautiful woman who represents

Columbia seated at the altar of Justice. As if from out of space there slowly appears a perfect and lifelike picture of Abraham Lincoln. The forming of the picture is first noticed by the appearance of what seems to be a mere spot on the front of the altar. This spot slowly enlarges and is focused into shape, until, to the amazement of the audience, the face of the great emancipator is clearly shown. President Lincoln's likeness is allowed to remain upon the altar just long enough for recognition, when, in the same mysterious manner that it appeared, it slowly fades and in its place there grows the picture of President Garfield. This in a like manner fades away, and again as out of the dim distance comes the picture of our great martyred president, William McKinley. The tableau is then dissolved into a picture of an assassin kneeling before the throne of Justice. Here the tableau ends, leaving an impression of mingled sorrow and sublimity upon the audience. . . .

McKINLEY'S LAST APPEARANCE

Chicago American, **September 15, 1901**

EDISON'S THE LAST PICTURES TAKEN . . .

LAST PUBLIC APPEARANCE OF MARTYR PRESIDENT SHOWN

To the Edison Manufacturing Company of Orange, N.J., of which Thomas A. Edison is the head, is due the credit of taking the pictures of President McKinley on the day of the assassination and which appeared in the *Chicago American* yesterday. Owing to an error the photographs having such a historical value were exposed as the work of the Neimeyer's Animatiscope Company, while they in fact were taken by an apparatus invented by Mr. Edison and for the company bearing his name.

On the last day that William McKinley appeared among his countrymen at the Buffalo exhibition the Edison Manufacturing Company prepared to take elaborate [moving] pictures by the kinetoscope during his address. Not only did this company secure the most successful photographs of President McKinley during his famous address, but a large number were secured of the surging crowd in its frantic excitement after the shooting of the President.

For all time to come these photographed scenes will have a value from a historical standpoint.

The pictures appearing in the *Chicago American* yesterday were taken under the supervision of James H. White of the Edison Manufacturing Company, and show the martyred President in many characteristic poses. They were probably secured some thirty minutes before the fatal visit to the Music Hall was made, and are among the last pictures taken of the President before he was stricken down. While many distinguished personages are shown in the group about the man marked for the bullet of the assassin, yet the central figure stands out clear and strong. The pictures taken by the wonderful kinetoscope show the President turning from right to left in addressing the great throng. . . .

TEN EDISON RECORDS BY WILLIAM JENNINGS BRYAN, 1908

Edison Phonograph Monthly, **June 1908**

We take great pleasure in announcing ten Edison Records by William Jennings Bryan.[5] They were made by the "Great Commoner" in the library of his home in Lincoln, Nebraska, one of our recording experts going there for the purpose. They are among the plainest and most natural Records we have ever turned out. No one who has ever heard Mr. Bryan speak will fail to recognize all of the wonderful charm of voice and manner for which he is famous.

Mr. Bryan needs no introduction. His prominence as the two-time and prospective third-time Democratic candidate for President, together with his remarkable gifts as an orator, have made him known everywhere, while his upright, Christian character and fearless exposition of his political beliefs stamp him as one of the foremost Americans of history.

The Records are composed of telling passages chosen by Mr. Bryan from his favorite orations. Hearing one of these tabloid addresses produces the same effect as a long speech from almost anyone else, so carefully has Mr. Bryan chosen his remarks.

In soliciting trade on these Records, Jobbers and Dealers should not fail to make it plain that the Records are made by Mr. Bryan himself and that they will appeal very strongly to women as well as men, as women always flock in large numbers to hear Mr. Bryan whenever he makes a public speech.

---

[5]William Jennings Bryan had lost to William McKinley in the presidential election of 1896. He lost to him again in 1900, and then ran (and lost) against William H. Taft in 1908.

The Bryan Records should go a long way towards offsetting the present trade dullness. We shall not be surprised if they outsell any set of Records we have ever issued, owing to Mr. Bryan's prominence in the current Presidential campaign.

9914 SWOLLEN FORTUNES

This is a subject of national interest that is likely to figure prominently in the coming Presidential campaign. Mr. Bryan favors active enforcement of the "Equal rights to all, special privileges to none" clause of the Bill of Rights, in order to secure a more equal distribution of the country's wealth. The reasons he advances for his views form a veritable gem of political logic. They are sure to cause wide discussion when Mr. Bryan takes the "stump" actively later on.

9915 THE LABOR QUESTION

In a thoroughly characteristic way Mr. Bryan upholds the fairness of the eight-hour day and arbitration of labor disputes. With equal vehemence he attacks government by injunction, which, he states, amounts to a practical denial of the laboring man's right to trial by jury. These are all live topics of the day and the Record will appeal especially to the laboring classes. . . .

9916 THE RAILROAD QUESTION

"Where does Bryan stand on the Railroad Question?" is being asked on all sides. He has been so widely, and in some cases, erroneously, quoted since his recent Madison Square Garden speech that the whole country has been waiting for an authoritative answer to their question. This record comes as his personal word on this important subject. It is certain to be in great demand.

9917 THE TRUST QUESTION

A brilliant exposition of the Bryan idea of trusts and trust evils, delivered with all of that rare enthusiasm with which the speaker is gifted. You may or may not share his political views, but must admit that none has ever shown a better mastery of the greatest problems of the day. He says, "Private monopolies can not be regulated by the government. We have tried that and the result was that monopolies regulated the government instead of being regulated by the government." He advocates extermination as the only practical remedy and brings the full measure of his persuasive eloquence into play to drive the point home.

9918 THE TARIFF QUESTION

"During the civil war," says Mr. Bryan, "the tariff was raised to carry on the war. It was continued after the war to allow our infant industries to stand on their feet. But it was not long until the 'infant industries' were standing not only on their own feet, but all over the feet of other people." A telling shot on the tariff. It is one of many delivered in his most vigorous style, for the tariff has always been a favorite subject with Mr. Bryan.

9919 POPULAR ELECTION OF SENATORS

Never is the commanding power of Bryan's eloquent logic shown off so favorably as when he strikes at some great legislative evil. He describes the popular election of Senators as "the most popular reform of the day.". . . This Record will appeal to all alike for, as Mr. Bryan points out, it is not a party question.

9920 IMPERIALISM

This is a subject on which Mr. Bryan never fails to delight his hearers. Territorial expansion will never want for a "fiery foe" so long as he is in the lists. "Our experiment in Colonialism has brought us not profit but loss," he says, and piles argument upon argument to show that he is in the right. He believes the retention of the Philippine Islands to be contrary to all American precedent and to the republican form of government, which derives its power from the consent of the governed. The climax of his address comes with an impassioned demand that the Filipinos be given their independence and allowed to work out their own destiny.

9921 GUARANTY OF BANK DEPOSITS

Here is a subject that is brimming with interest because it outlines the much-discussed Bryan remedy for the banking troubles through which the country has just passed. "The Government demands protection on its own deposits," says he. "Why should not private individuals have equal protection?" This Record also treats of a live political issue and the Record will undoubtedly be very popular.

9922 AN IDEAL REPUBLIC

Perhaps no American of to-day can equal Mr. Bryan in the difficult dual art of conceiving ideal conditions and finding suitable language for describing them. . . . "Behold a Republic," he exclaims, "where every citizen is a sovereign, but none cares to wear a crown; whose flag is love while others' is only fear." His peroration is very fine and concludes with these words, "A Republic, whose history, like the path of the just, is as the shining light that shineth more and more unto the perfect day."

9923 IMMORTALITY

This Record consists of selections from Mr. Bryan's best known lyceum lecture, "The Prince of Peace." Mrs. Bryan likes it best of all his addresses. We do not recall having heard a more affecting description of supreme faith in a "life beyond." Mr. Bryan is evidently as profound a thinker upon such questions as upon those affecting the country's political welfare. . . .

TEN EDISON RECORDS BY WILLIAM HOWARD TAFT, 1908

Edison Phonograph Monthly, **September 1908**

William H. Taft, Republican candidate for President, has made . . . Edison Records. The records consist of the most striking portions of his Speech of Acceptance, which was delivered at Cincinnati, July 28th.

As Mr. Taft says, the Records give his "personal views on the leading political questions." And, we may add that they do this in a wonderfully lucid and concise manner.

They are splendidly recorded in Mr. Taft's most amiable voice and do full justice to the distinguished Ohioan's oratorical powers.

Now, for the first time, one can introduce the rival candidates for the Presidency in one's own home, can listen to their political views, expressed in their real voices, and make comparisons . . .

9996 FOREIGN MISSIONS

Mr. Taft's views on the importance of foreign missions are here crystallized into a model sermonette. As the representative of this country, Mr. Taft spent much time in the Orient and had an unusual opportunity for studying his subject at close range. "It was not until then," says he, "that I realized the immense importance of foreign missions to the spread of civilization." This record will probably stand as the ablest and most impartial exposition of this great subject. . . .

9997 IRISH HUMOR

This delightful talk on an every-day subject is certain to be very popular. It is of the after-dinner type, at which Mr. Taft has no superior, and is delivered in his most affable voice. "A sense of humor," says the speaker, "is like the bumpers in a solid train ... it saves the jolt. ..." He then repeats an apt and beautiful quotation from John Boyle O'Reilly and another from Kipling's poem, "An American.". . .

9998 REPUBLICAN AND DEMOCRATIC TREATMENT OF TRUSTS

On the day after Mr. Taft delivered his powerful "Speech of Acceptance" the whole country was aroused by the newspaper reports of his remarkable allusion to the Trusts. . . . "Unlawful trusts should be restrained with all the efficiency of injunctive progress. And the persons engaged in maintaining them should be punished with all the severity of criminal prosecution. . . . This is the Republican view. . . ."

9999 THE RIGHTS OF LABOR

A great battle is now being fought by the leading political parties on the labor question. Mr. Bryan's Edison Record on this subject led all of his other Records in sales. Now we have the chance to compare Messrs. Taft and Bryan's personal views. . . . Mr. Taft's compelling argument in favor of labor unions is one that will find an enthusiastic echo in the heart of every union man. . . .

10000 UNLAWFUL TRUSTS

So important does Mr. Taft consider this subject that he decided to discuss it in a special Record. He rises to the heights of true eloquence in denouncing monopolies that seek to control the market, raise prices, and drive out competition. At the same time he makes it quite plain that legitimate business organization is needed to make possible reasonable prices and to promote prosperity.

10001 FUNCTION OF THE NEXT ADMINISTRATION

One of the most engaging subjects Mr. Taft could have chosen. He pays a glowing tribute to the high standards of business operation forced upon the corporations and large business firms by President Roosevelt. He recites the most important ones and says, "the chief function of the next administration in my judgement, is to complete and perfect the machinery by which these high standards of Roosevelt may be maintained, by which law-breakers may be restrained and punished, but which shall operate with sufficient accuracy and dispatch as to interfere with legitimate business as little as possible. . . ."

10003 PHILIPPINES

Without question Mr. Taft is better qualified to inform us about the Philippines than any other American. He was sent there by the U.S. Government at the most critical time in the Islands' history—just after the Spanish war—and was largely instrumental in establishing law and order out of chaos. He tells just what has already been accomplished there and asserts his belief that the Islands should be made independent when the people are able to govern themselves. This he thinks will take two generations. A splendid peroration is concluded with these ringing words, "It would be cowardly to lay down the burden until our purpose is accomplished."

10004 ENFORCED INSURANCE ON BANK DEPOSITS

This is the great national political question brought up by the recent business disturbance. It will be highly interesting to compare Messrs. Taft and Bryan's Records on this subject. Mr. Taft opposes in his most vigorous fashion the Democratic idea of government guaranty of bank deposits. "The idea is wholly impracticable," he says, "unless it is to be accompanied by a revolution in our banking system. If the proposal were adopted as proposed, it would break the whole banking system down in ruins. . . ."

10006 THE FARMER AND THE REPUBLICAN PARTY

This Record will make a powerful special appeal to those who live in the country districts. Mr. Taft enters fully into those subjects that are of first importance to every farmer, such as restraint of excessive railroad rates, enforcement of the pure food law, scientific agriculture, and increasing the comforts of the country life by the extension of the rural free delivery and building of good country roads, more and more at the public expense and less at that of the abutting property owner. No farmer or subordinate, who is interested in these matters can afford to forego hearing Mr. Taft's personal word on the subject.

10007 RIGHTS AND PROGRESS OF THE NEGRO

While the South is the center of interest on the Negro question, still it is becoming more than ever a matter of national concern. If anything, Mr. Taft is more vehement in declaring his position on this question than on any other. Alluding to the declaration of the Republican Party in favor of the 13th, 14th, and 15th amendments, and justice to all men without regard to race or color, Mr. Taft says, "It is needless to state that I stand with my party squarely on that plank of the platform."

Mass Media and Their Markets

Despite Edison's early and extraordinary successes with both recorded sound and motion pictures, his phonograph and film companies did not continue to make millions as the twentieth century progressed. There were many causes for their decline, of course, among them competition in the field and the outcome of extensive patent litigation. One fundamental cause, however, may have been that Edison and the men he hired as corporate managers failed to accommodate themselves to a new kind of market that was emerging in America. This new market was driven with a new intensity by public taste, by mercurial appetites for the latest stars and the greatest hits, and by companies adapted to take advantage of change. The policy statement and correspondence included here help to document Edison's less flexible strategies. His missteps in the field of recorded sound are suggested by the fact that he himself continued to decide which artists and which "tunes" (as he called all musical selections) should be recorded and released. This despite the fact that he had no musical training and was increasingly hard of hearing. He filled notebook after notebook with his pass-fail critiques. In one he wrote of the young Al Jolson: "Coney Island saloon singer. Not for us." He was known to disparage the great Sergei Rachmaninov as "a pounder" on the piano.

By comparison, Edison had much less direct control over film production by the Edison Manufacturing Company. Yet there too his misreadings of the modern marketplace are suggestive. In 1911 he announced a new addition to his film business, an educational film division. He saw the popularity of nickelodeons across the country and wanted to capitalize on that popularity to the betterment of American society. Why not teach with movies? The films described here all share a Progressive sensibility with which Edison generally agreed.

EDISON'S POLICY FOR MAKING RECORDS AND RELATED CORRESPONDENCE, 1912, 1914–1915

Policy Statement, May 11, 1912

Policy [handwritten by Edison]:

1st we care nothing for the reputation of the artist, singer, or instrumentalist, except in a few rare instances where the person has established a unique & isolated position.

2. All that we desire is that the voice shall be as perfect as possible, free of conspicuous tremulo, clear and without ragged sustained notes, free of subsidiary & false waves on these notes. [We want] singers who can sustain their pitch so as to be used in concerted work, who have sufficient overtones to produce mellow & not sharp mechanical tones. Singers whose volume changes are violent & ill judged, so it makes it difficult to record are not wanted.

3. When good voices are found to exclusively contract 1 or 2 years with the option to extend, pay a regular salary for a determined and known portion of their daily time, taking in view their other engagements.

4. To discover these good voices that we can build up a body of good singers, Bassos, Baritones, Tenors, & corresponding female voices, so we can have a soloist for any tune & concert, any tune or part of an opera, also special voices for comic work.

5. To have a recording man who will travel countries, make trials of voices at singing schools, local opera houses etc & submit the voice to Edison for a while until the system is established & to keep this hunt up constantly.

6. All tunes which are to be used on the phonograph except the local topical songs which are fleeting are to be entered in the tune book, each tune to be rated as to its desirability & none others used.

7. Where artists are engaged to execute a definite number of pieces, they are to submit their repertoire & we must judge as to the tunes we want. If we cannot find enough in their repertoire, then we submit our list of tunes to see if any of these can be executed by the artist; if not, we do not want him or her.

8. Any new tune that is published which is melodious & which seems to have merit enough & is of such a character that gives a promise of sustained popularity over a long period should be sent to Orange to be judged to see if worthy to be put in the tune book.

9. No engagements of any kind to be entered into with artists whose voice has not been sent to Orange & judged.

10. It is not our intention to feature artists or sell the record by using the artists' names except in few instances. We intend to rely entirely upon the tune & the high quality of the voices & not on names of the artists.

11. With a regular corps of singers we will be enabled to rehearse, change the voices and style of accompaniments and make several duplicates of the tune & thus adopt the most perfect one. A couple of the best types of the tune as executed can be sent to Orange & masters made, from these the most satisfactory one can be selected. We will not object to making these extra masters providing we can get higher quality in execution.

Edison to Santa Fe Watch Company, November 11, 1914

TOPEKA, KANSAS

Gentlemen:
Your favor of the 21st instant has been handed to me, and I have read it with a great deal of interest.

Has it occurred to you that records salable in one part of the Country are entirely unsalable in another part? We get a variety of requests from all over the Country. From New England we get violent protests against putting on ragtime and Coon Songs. Up there they want operas and orchestra selections, together with dance records for the factory people. The Broadway hits do not sell there.

In Dakota they want Band records. This is true also of Southern Ohio, Kentucky and Tennessee. All these demands are backed up by sarcastic letters, all of which are very discouraging, in fact so much so that if I had known that there was such a wide difference of opinion about music, I would never have had anything to do with it. Sometimes I wish I were out of it altogether. All I can say is that we will do the best we can to satisfy these conflicting requests.

Yours very truly,
Thomas A. Edison

Edison to Harger & Blish, February 8, 1915

DES MOINES, IOWA

Gentlemen:

Your friend of the Santa Fe Watch [Company] is a very critical person. However, I want criticisms, although it is some work to explain, but in this case I will try to make my ideas and policies clear.

1st. I am more interested in good mechanisms, and especially in good reproducers than in cabinets. I neglect cabinets. If your friend only knew how many reproducers were discarded and changed . . . he would see that we don't get results without great expense, and that I prefer good machinery to high grade furniture. . . .

2nd. He talks about the label. There is no known material that will stick to the substance of which the records are made, and I'll bet I have tried two thousand things. Again, out of forty pigments and one hundred and twenty-six Aniline dyes not a single one retained its color after it has passed though the 360 degrees of heat in the press.

3rd. Of course, you will be asked frequently about Caruso, Melba, Scotti [and other famous opera singers] on the Edison [label]. About every dealer I know of says he states to inquirers that if they buy an Edison machine they can use an attachment and buy and play any kind of record, but the public don't [sic] seem to hanker after these high grade artists of the Victor [label] after they have bought the attachment.

With the exception of Caruso, nearly every Grand Opera artist got their reputation not by their voice but by personality, by acting, and the glamour of the stage. We cannot use the eye with the phonograph, hence only Grand Opera singers with good voices can be used, and I have nearly all of them. I am not going to queer the Diamond Disc [Edison records] by a poor singer, no matter what their reputation in Opera may be. Let me say that Scotti has lost his voice almost entirely, but because he is one of the best actors on the Operatic Stage and a great favorite, am I to have him sing on the phonograph merely on account of his great reputation? I prefer that the Victor should do this. Why don't [sic] Melba sing for the Opera and get the $1500 per night she once obtained? The explanation is simple. Her voice has faded, but that don't [sic] phase the Victor [Talking Machine Company] because their entire business has been built on advertising Grand Opera Singers, who in the case of the best known, got their reputation

"Looking for the Band" (1901) Strategies for the sale of musical phonographs and records varied. This advertisement stresses the "realism" of a "genuine" Edison. It is clear that Edison clung too long to acoustic fidelity as his chief selling point, while other manufacturers realized that consumers wanted to hear star performers and the latest hits.
Courtesy of the Edison National Historic Site, National Park Service, U.S. Department of the Interior.

by acting. I shall not follow this method of selling goods because, in the long run, I do not think it will win. . . .

The price he says should be on the face of the record. How does he know that there might not be some very good reason why it should not be on? I can go into lengthy explanations as to this, but there is a good technical reason or I should have put it on. I should be credited in cases like this with as much intelligence as the general average of the genus *homo*.

I return the letter of the Santa Fe Watch Company.

Yours very truly,
Thomas A. Edison

Edison to F. R. Humphries, June 28, 1915

WEST PHILADELPHIA, PA.

Dear Sir:
Now and then we get a letter from a music lover, like yourself, and it grieves us exceedingly to find ourselves in the position we are. If we put out much high-class music, we are immediately bombarded with letters from every dealer, from the Atlantic to the Pacific, to "stop it" "Can't sell it" "Cut out the high brow stuff," etc. As a matter of fact, the sales are small compared with those of the so-called popular records. We have investigated this matter thoroughly to see if we could ascertain the reason and we find that the principal reason is that the younger members of the average phonograph owner's family wants only records of what are termed popular selections. . . .

Very truly yours,
Thomas A. Edison

FIVE EDISON FILMS OF THE PROGRESSIVE ERA, 1912

(1) No. 6943   Released Jan. 3, 1912   About 995 feet

The Two Flats

CAST OF CHARACTERS

THE IRISH WIDOW	Alice Washburn
HER SON	Edward Boulden
THE ITALIAN WIDOWER	Charles M. Seay
HIS DAUGHTER	Jeanie McPhearson

This story depicts the funny side of life in the tenement house district.
An Irish widow moves into a flat and proceeds to arrange her household, doing considerable hammering, to the great annoyance of an Italian widower who lives directly underneath. A lively discussion ensues through the open windows, both claiming individual rights for the rent they pay. The widow writes her son to come home and protect her from the "insulting Dago down-stairs," while the Italian writes his daughter to come home and comfort him, as an Irish widow has

---

From *The Kinetophone,* published by Thomas A. Edison, Incorporated, 1912

moved in up-stairs who makes him sick. Her son and his daughter start home and become acquainted at the railroad station, but neither knows where the other lives. Meanwhile the hilarious war between the widow and the Italian continues. In sprinkling her flowers on the window-sill the water splashes into his room below. He retaliates by knocking her flower pots off the sill with the aid of a broom and she wrenches the broom from his grasp. A little later she shakes the crumbs from the table cover out through the window and he yanks the dangling cloth out of her hands. Now he has her table cover and she has his broom.

The Italian explains the situation to his daughter, who has just arrived home. She starts up-stairs to return the widow's table cover, while the son goes down-stairs with the "Dago's" broom. They meet in the hallway and are surprised to find that they both live in the same house. They form a great liking for each other and frequently signal one another from their windows. On one such occasion he drops a bouquet from his window to the girl; the Italian gets it, and thinking it is a peace offering from the widow, he immediately goes upstairs to pay his respects, and they become good friends.

A comical mishap causing a crash of china and glass-ware brings their respective son and daughter into the room. After due explanations the scene terminates happily in typical East Side fashion.

(2) No. 6981   Released February 23, 1912   1000 feet

Children Who Labor By Ethel Browning

Produced in cooperation with the National Child Labor Committee

CAST OF CHARACTERS

MR. HANSCOMB, a large mill owner	Robert Conness
HIS WIFE	Miriam Nesbitt
THEIR LITTLE GIRL	Leonine Flugrath
A FOREIGNER UNABLE TO OBTAIN WORK	John Sturgeon
HIS WIFE	Mary Fuller
THEIR CHILDREN	Viola Flugrath

. . . The subject of child labor in the United States is one that is being constantly discussed. The intensely interesting story, which this film tells, carries a theme which ought to appeal strongly to every thinking man, woman, and child in the country.

Beginning with a remarkable symbolic scene of toiling masses of children on their way to the deadening work in the mills, the story unfolds itself by making us first acquainted with a situation which few people realize; men being thrown out of their employment while children are taken from schools and from play to do work. . . .

A foreigner who does not understand the ways of this country applies for work at a mill, but is sent away with the intimation that if he has a child that there will be work for it, but none for himself. We then travel in vision to New York to the home of a wealthy mill owner to whom an appeal is being made to use his influence against child labor. He indicates that he can do nothing about it and resents the insinuation that his own child might be one of the unfortunates except for her birth and his protection. His wife shows her interest in the project.

We turn to the mill again and find that the foreigner, pushed by his poverty and unable to get work himself, finally yields and puts his little daughter to work, as the family must have food.

The next thing we see is that Hanscomb, the rich mill owner has sent his wife and child on a journey, and the little one, getting off the train in a spirit of mischief, is left behind in a small town which happens to be the same one in which the foreigner, aforementioned, and his family live. The child is found by them, and as they cannot understand each other, his kindly wife takes her home and shares her poor cottage with her.

Of course Hanscomb and his wife are frantic and put detectives to work on the case, but without success.

Meanwhile things go badly with the foreigner and he feels that it is necessary to put the little stranger to work with his own child. Then Hanscomb buys the mill and so unconsciously becomes the employer of his own child. Going down to look over the new property, he enters the mill just as his own child has fainted and is carried out by her little companions, and so he misses her. She is carried past her own mother at the gate and Mrs. Hanscomb, touched by the incident, though not knowing, of course, who the strange child is, gets her address and in the evening goes there with the footman with a basket of food for the little sufferer.

Of course, there is a reunion, Mr. Hanscomb is sent for and finds that his little daughter has learned a lesson that he has not as yet. She refuses to be taken away by herself and pleads that all the other little children be set free from slavery. He is unable to refuse her request, and the film story closes with better conditions put into effect, though we are reminded at the end that the condition called "Child Labor" still exists and demands our attention.

Photographically and dramatically, the film is superb and supplemented by the wide magazine publicity given the subject and the work of the National Child Labor Committee, it ought to prove one of the biggest features. . . .

(3) No. 6997   Released Mar. 15, 1912
About 1000 Feet

For the Commonwealth

Produced in Co-operation with National Committee on Prison Labor

CAST OF CHARACTERS

AN UNSKILLED LABORER ....Barry O'Moore
HIS WIFE ....Mary Fuller
THEIR CHILD...Edna May Weick
GOVERNOR OF THE STATE...Robert Brower
WARDEN OF THE PRISON ....Charles Ogle

A young man, unskilled and out of work, deserts his family and upon being arrested for this desertion, assaults an officer and for this last offense, is sent to State Prison, while his wife tries to support herself and her child by shirt making.

The enforced idleness of confinement is so terrible to the convicts that the warden, out of common humanity, asks the governor to sanction some employment for them. They are accordingly taught shirt making and thus the husband in prison becomes the competitor of his wife outside the walls. Prison labor is cheap and of course it puts her out of business and she is forced to take refuge in the State Poor House. Meanwhile the governor receives a protest from the girl shirt makers who have been thrown out of employment by his new plan for the convicts and he is in a quandary as to what to do. Upon visiting the poor house, however, he is informed by a little child who happens to be the child of our particular friend, the convict, that she needs new shoes and he finds that the State appropriation is not sufficient to afford these things for his own institutions. A solution of his great problem thus suggests itself to him and the change is accordingly made at the State Prison, the men being taught the trade of shoe making and the product of their labor being used entirely by the state and not in the open market in competition with Free Labor.

Of course, by this change our hero becomes a skilled laborer instead of merely "a man of muscle," and when he makes his exit from the penitentiary he is able to apply at the same shoe factory, from which we first saw him turned away, and get employment. The picture closes with a reunion of the little family after their terrible experiences and the scene brings a heart throb because of its simplicity.

(4) No. 7104   Released August 24, 1912
About 1000 feet

The War on the Mosquito

Some smile and some [even] say "graft" when they read of the annual appropriations by our state and countries to fight the mosquito. But this is unjust as the work is of great value to the public health. In New Jersey, our most prominent mosquito state, thousands of dollars are being expended annually to drain the salt marshes and stagnant inland pools where mosquitoes breed. Essex county in that state alone has appropriated seventy-five thousand dollars for mosquito extermination in nineteen hundred and twelve. In other sections of our country similar work is going on. For instance the extermination of the yellow Fever and Malarial mosquito in the canal zone has been the principal means of making the Panama Canal possible.

The picture entitled "The War on the Mosquito" presents in a clear, intensely interesting and instructive way just how this work is being conducted. Both the salt marsh and inland work are shown in detail. The places where mosquitoes breed; the different means of treatment to prevent same, and the machines used in the work make a complete picture in themselves. In addition to these interesting views of the work in the field we have been able to produce some very remarkable pictures of the life history of the mosquito itself, showing in minute detail its development from the egg to the larva, from the larva to the pupa, and the actual hatching from the pupa to the adult mosquito. Here also we have been able to show the natural enemies devouring the mosquito while in their water stage, finally concluding the picture by showing a greatly enlarged mosquito biting a man's hand.

Besides being of great instructive value, this picture will be of great interest to any and every audience.

(5) No. 7158   Released Oct. 30, 1912
About 600 feet

A Suffragette in Spite of Himself

CAST OF CHARACTERS

A GENTLEMAN OPPOSED
    TO WOMAN'S SUFFRAGE...................................Marc MacDermott
HIS WIFE..Miriam Nesbitt
THE MAID ....Ethel Browning

Women at the suffrage meeting and anti-suffragists.
This is a comedy built around a subject which is at present the chief
one of the day in England and hardly less important in this country.
How a thoroughly respectable British householder, bitterly opposed to
woman's suffrage, becomes apparently a violent advocate of the cause,
the difficulties this gets him into finally leading to his arrest, his
forcible rescue by a band of suffragettes who believe him their cham-
pion, his final arrival home in a torn and dilapidated condition before
his astonished wife, and above all, how the fatal "votes for women"
confronts him at the end—all these make the fun fast and furious. It
can well be imagined that in such capable hands the leading parts
leave nothing to be desired.

The picture is entirely played in London and the appropriate street
backgrounds (including the famous Trafalgar Square) add greatly to
its value.

A Thomas A. Edison Chronology (1847–1931)

1847 Born February 11

1861–
1865 American Civil War

1869 Applies for his first patent, on an electric vote recorder

1871 Marries sixteen-year-old Mary Stilwell

1873 Financial depression or "panic"

1876 Moves to his new laboratory at Menlo Park, New Jersey

1877 Invention of the phonograph

1878 Announces that he will make incandescent electric lighting successful

1882 Opens Pearl Street central power station in New York's financial district

1886 Marries second wife, Mina Miller

1887 Moves into newly constructed laboratory at West Orange, New Jersey

1888 Begins manufacture of his "perfected" phonograph in West Orange

1889 Begins motion picture experiments, conducted by W. K. L. Dickson and others

1894 Public demonstration of "peephole" kinetoscope motion picture machines

1896 Experiments to exploit x-rays, inventing the "fluoroscope"

1900 Obtains U.S. trademark for his signature; occupied with experimental pursuit and manufacture of Portland cement and alkaline storage batteries

1904 Former employee Clarence Dally dies of (x-ray) radiation burns

1911 Consolidates sales and manufacturing companies as Thomas A. Edison, Incorporated

1914– World War I
1918

1915 Named to U.S. Naval Consulting Board; manufactures organic chemicals to make up for loss of German supply during war

1923 Begins efforts to find a domestic source for rubber, eventually supported by Henry Ford and Harvey Firestone

1929 "Diamond Jubilee" of the electric light

1931 Dies October 18

Questions for Consideration

1. What is the relationship between technology and progress? Does technology always advance? Are certain advances or their sequence inevitable? Think of examples.

2. Is "invention" a term or concept applicable to today's computer technology? Why not, or in what ways?

3. View some of the earliest Edison motion pictures at the Library of Congress's American Memory Project Web site <memory.loc.gov>. Can you generalize about the form and subject matter of early films? Do some of the same film genres still exist today?

4. Visit the Thomas A. Edison Papers digital edition at <edison.rutgers.edu>. Select the clippings collection and examine some of the articles from the period 1878 to 1898. With what terms were competing technologies compared? Was invention understood as an event or process? Was individual rather than the collaborative effort emphasized? What social characteristics were assigned to inventors, engineers, investors, and manufacturers?

5. Judging from the documents in chapter 1, what kind of person was Edison? How can you tell?

6. Judging from the documents in chapter 2, what can accounts of the phonograph in 1878 reveal about the cultural authority of speaking at that time? Why might people have been so sure that the phonograph would be a device for "capturing" speech rather than for playing music? What kinds of speech and what sorts of speakers seemed most important to capture and why?

7. Edison claimed that the phonograph was his only accidental invention. Do you believe him? Why or why not?

8. Based on the documents in chapter 3, how do different primary sources agree or disagree about how—or even when—Edison's incandescent lamp succeeded?

9. American homes now have electricity, but many also have natural gas appliances. People may own computers, but they probably do not also own typewriters. What accounts for the varying degrees of social commitment to different technologies?

10. Based on the documents in chapter 4, how did the new media of the 1890s help to change perceptions of the "real" world? Do similar conditions pertain to the new media of today? How is technology asked to solve social problems? In what ways have these documents altered your thoughts about cultural diversity?

11. Edison's method of pouring whole concrete houses worked. Why don't more of us live in poured houses?

12. Which among Edison's legacies are the most enduring? Where is he most evident in the twenty-first century?

Selected Bibliography

WORKS ON THOMAS EDISON

Baldwin, Neil. *Edison: Inventing the Century.* New York: Hyperion, 1995.

Bazerman, Charles. *The Languages of Edison's Light.* Cambridge, Mass.: MIT Press, 1999.

Friedel, Robert and Paul Israel with Bernard S. Finn. *Edison's Electric Light: Biography of an Invention.* New Brunswick, NJ: Rutgers University Press, 1986.

Israel, Paul. *Edison: A Life of Invention.* New York: John Wiley & Sons, 1998.

Millard, A. J. *Edison and the Business of Innovation.* Baltimore: Johns Hopkins University Press, 1990.

Melosi, Martin V. *Thomas A. Edison and the Modernization of America.* Edited by Oscar Handlin. New York: HarperCollins, 1990.

Nye, David E. *The Invented Self: An Anti-Biography, from Documents of Thomas A. Edison.* Odense, Denmark: Odense University Press, 1983.

Peterson, Michael. "Thomas Edison's Concrete House," *Invention and Technology* 11 (Winter 1996): 50–56.

Pretzer, William S., ed. *Working at Inventing: Thomas Edison and the Menlo Park Experience.* Dearborn, Mich.: Henry Ford Museum and Greenfield Village, 1989.

Reynolds, Terry, and Theodore Bernstein. "Edison and 'The Chair'" *IEEE Technology and Society Magazine* 8 (1989): 19–28.

Thulesius, Olav. *Edison in Florida: The Green Laboratory.* Gainesville: University Press of Florida, 1997.

Wachhorst, Wyn. *Thomas Alva Edison: An American Myth.* Cambridge, Mass.: MIT Press, 1981.

PRIMARY SOURCES AND REFERENCE MATERIAL
ON THOMAS EDISON

Jeffrey, Thomas E. et al., eds. *The Thomas A. Edison Papers, A Selective Microfilm Edition.* Multiple parts. Bethesda: University Publications of America, 1985 and ongoing.

Jenkins, Reese V. et al., eds. *The Papers of Thomas A. Edison.* Multiple volumes. Baltimore: Johns Hopkins University Press, 1989 and ongoing.

The Motion Pictures and Sound Recordings of the Edison Companies. American Memory: Historical Collections for the National Digital Library. Library of Congress. 1999. <http://memory.loc.gov/ammem/edhtml/edhome.html>.

Musser, Charles. *Edison Motion Pictures, 1890–1900: An Annotated Filmography.* Gemona, Italy: Le Giornate del Cinema Muto; Washington, D.C.: Smithsonian Institution Press, 1997.

The Thomas A. Edison Papers. Ongoing Digital Edition. Thomas A. Edison Papers Project. Rutgers, The State University of New Jersey, 2000. <http://edison.rutgers.edu>.

RELATED WORKS ON TECHNOLOGICAL CHANGE

Bijker, Wiebe E. *Of Bicycles, Bakelites, and Bulbs: Toward a Theory of Sociotechnical Change.* Cambridge, Mass.: MIT Press, 1995.

Cowan, Ruth Schwartz. *More Work for Mother: The Ironies of Household Technology from the Open Hearth to the Microwave.* New York: Basic Books, 1983.

———. *A Social History of American Technology.* New York: Oxford University Press, 1997.

Hughes, Thomas P. *Networks of Power: Electrification in Western Society, 1880–1930.* Baltimore: Johns Hopkins University Press, 1983.

Kirsch, David A. *The Electric Car and the Burden of History.* New Brunswick: Rutgers University Press, 2000.

Kittler, Friedrich A. *Gramophone, Film, Typewriter.* Translated by Geoffrey Winthrop-Young and Michael Wutz. Stanford: Stanford University Press, 1999.

Kline, Ronald R. *Consumers in the Country: Technology and Social Change in Rural America.* Baltimore: Johns Hopkins University Press, 2000.

Lubar, Steven D. *InfoCulture: The Smithsonian Book of Information Age Inventions.* Boston: Houghton Mifflin, 1993.

Marvin, Carolyn. *When Old Technologies Were New: Thinking about Electric Communication in the Late Nineteenth Century.* New York: Oxford University Press, 1988.

Musser, Charles. *Before the Nickelodeon: Edwin S. Porter and the Edison Manufacturing Company.* Berkeley: University of California Press, 1991.

———. *The Emergence of Cinema: The American Screen to 1907.* New York: Charles Scribner's Sons, 1990.

Nye, David E. *Electrifying America: Social Meanings of a New Technology, 1880–1940.* Cambridge, Mass.: MIT Press, 1990.

Schiffer, Michael Brian. *Taking Charge: The Electric Automobile in America.* Washington, D.C.: Smithsonian Institution Press, 1994.

Tenner, Edward. *Why Things Bite Back: Technology and the Revenge of Unintended Consequences.* New York: Alfred A. Knopf, 1996.

Index